YOUR KNOWLEDGE H

Bibliographic information published by the German National Library:

The German National Library lists this publication in the National Bibliography; detailed bibliographic data are available on the Internet at http://dnb.dnb.de .

Imprint:

Copyright © 2019 GRIN Verlag
Print and binding: Books on Demand GmbH, Norderstedt Germany
ISBN: 9783346225146

This book at GRIN:

https://www.grin.com/document/900562

Juliet Adjei

Effects of Financing on Solid Waste Management at the Local Level

A Case Study of Kumasi Metropolis

GRIN Verlag

GRIN - Your knowledge has value

Since its foundation in 1998, GRIN has specialized in publishing academic texts by students, college teachers and other academics as e-book and printed book. The website www.grin.com is an ideal platform for presenting term papers, final papers, scientific essays, dissertations and specialist books.

Visit us on the internet:

http://www.grin.com/

http://www.facebook.com/grincom

http://www.twitter.com/grin_com

KWAME NKRUMAH UNIVERSITY OF SCIENCE AND TECHNOLOGY, KUMASI GHANA

EFFECTS OF FINANCING ON SOLID WASTE MANAGEMENT AT THE LOCAL LEVEL: A CASE STUDY OF KUMASI METROPOLIS

BY

JULIET ADJEI (BA. INTEGRATED DEVELOPMENT STUDIES)

A THESIS SUBMITTED TO THE DEPARTMENT OF PLANNING,
COLLEGE OF ART AND BUILT ENVIRONMENT
IN PARTIAL FULFILLMENT OF THE REQUIREMENTS FOR THE DEGREE

MASTER OF SCIENCE
IN DEVELOPMENT PLANNING AND MANAGEMENT

JUNE, 2019

ABSTRACT

Solid waste management is one of the major challenging issues in developing countries. The study identified the effects of financing on solid waste management in the Kumasi metropolis. Purposive sampling technique was used in this work. Whiles multiple instruments were employed for the data collection. The respondents were basically staff of the Metropolitan Assembly's waste management department, staff of Private Waste Management Companies, Individual solid waste collectors, Bus terminal operators/Managers and Market users/hawkers. In all, a total number of Seventy-one (71) respondents were interviewed. It was discovered that all actors have very high level of commitment to achieving a sustainable solid waste management. However, the low level of technical and financial capacity of actors coupled with other factors impedes their operations. The total cost burden of solid waste management in the metropolis is shared among the KMA, private waste management companies and the clients. The KMA receives financial support from some foreign organisations, tipping fees at the landfill site and tricycle operators' charges for disposal while private waste management companies are financed through service charges, loans from financial institutions and other investments by the companies. However, clients' unwillingness to pay charges as well as high cost of private waste management company's operations does not help them financially. High dumping charges also deter people from dumping at sanitary sites and securing a bin which resort to indiscriminate dumping. To help mobilise, access and manage available funds for solid waste management, generated waste should be given value by the KMA and waste management companies to pay for its management resources. Clients must be educated on the importance of payment for service delivery by the KMA. While accessing funds, the companies must also deliver quality services which will entice clients to pay the charged fees and be ready to accept any future increment in fee paying. Companies should invest their profits in other profitable sectors in relation to environmental conservation through waste management to boost their financial strength. Finally, the Assembly should support the private waste management companies in charge of clean up, waste collection and disposal in the commercial areas financially to employ more people to undertake clean up exercises and acquire more logistics for waste collection and disposal.

ACKNOWLEDGEMENTS

I thank the Almighty God for his divine supply, guidance and protection throughout this course. May His wondrous name be praised.

My profound gratitude to my academic supervisor Dr. Kafui Ocloo for her patience, encouragement and guidance throughout the study.

To all lecturers at the Department of Planning especially Dr. Eric Oduro Ofori for his selfless guidance. God bless you all.

My interminable gratitude to my parents Sadick Adjei and Victoria Boakye for their financial assistance, prayers and encouragements. May the good Lord bless and keep you.

My appreciation also goes to all the people who made this research possible especially, the head of research department of the Kumasi Waste Management, Operations manager of various private waste management companies in Kumasi; Zoomlion Ghana Limited, Kumasi Waste Limited, SAK-M Waste management Limited and Asadu Royal Seed and Waste Management Limited; the managers of bus terminals and the heads of market associations. God bless you all.

DEDICATION

I dedicate this work to my Mother and all my cherished sponsors for their immerse efforts and contribution towards my study making this achievement possible. God richly bless you all.

TABLE OF CONTENTS

LIST OF TABLES

LIST OF FIGURES

LIST OF PLATES

LIST OF ACRONYMS

CBD's	–	Central Business Districts
EHMD	–	Environmental Health Management Department
EHSD	–	Environmental Health and Sanitation Department
GEPA	–	Ghana Environmental Protection Agency
ISWA	–	International Solid Waste Association.
ISWM	–	Integrated Solid Waste Management
KMA	–	Kumasi Metropolitan Assembly
KMA-WMD	–	Kumasi Metropolitan Waste Management Department
KWMD	–	Kumasi Waste Management Department
MMDA's	–	Metropolitan, Municipal and District Assemblies
MSWM	–	Municipal Solid Waste Management
UNEP	–	United Nation Environmental Programme
USEPA	–	United States Environmental Protection Agency
USPS	–	Urban Sector Programme Support Secretariat
WMD	–	Waste Management Department

CHAPTER ONE

GENERAL INTRODUCTION

1.0 BACKGROUND OF THE STUDY

Poor sanitation is a common environmental issue in developing countries as compared to developed countries and the issue is not different from local communities in Ghana. In Ghana, high income areas are characterised by clean environments while low income communities are characterised by abhorrent stench from heaps of waste and choked drains especially around highly populated and congested areas, market centres, busy transit areas and slums (Monney et al., 2013). This indicates that the filth in which we find ourselves now is highly dependent on the widespread poverty among the populace.

Solid waste management has over the years been a disturbing issue for city authorities in Ghana, particularly in Accra and Kumasi; where over 4,000tons of solid waste is generated daily in varied proportion to these cities (Monney et al., 2013). Waste management departments continuously struggle with the collection of huge amount of solid waste and the capacity of the authorities has been greatly overwhelmed by the ever-increasing amounts of waste at urban centres (Monney et al., 2013). This presents a host of health and environmental problems as these huge piles of waste pose grave risks to human life.

In Kumasi Metropolitan Assembly, central waste bins are designated at places for public use and constitute 58.8%; followed by house to house collection 17.2% mostly characterised by residential areas with organised streets, structures and environment; and finally public dump (open space) constitutes 15.6% (GSS, 2014) which include dumping on open fields, backyards and bushes amongst others which indicates that communal waste collection system is utilised more (GSS, 2014).

1.1 PROBLEM STATEMENT

Inadequate finance for solid waste management results in poor sanitation issues. In terms of waste management, Ghanaians have different perception as compared to the Singaporean and Philippinos which is a great challenge since Ghanaians regard all forms of solid waste to be fated for the landfill site (Monney et al., 2013). Waste management companies, which are supposed to benefit from converting useful resources in the solid waste stream into valuable products, have become waste collection companies (Monney

1

et al., 2013). However, solid waste management goes far beyond collection and disposing-off at landfill site. It deals with the control of generation, storage, collection, transfer and transport, processing and disposal conforming to the best principles of public health, economics, engineering, conservation, aesthetics and other environmental conditions (Tchobanoglous, 2003). In view of this financing and source of fund for waste management is crucial.

Ghana is faced with a great challenge in sanitation issue in public and residential areas. Despite outsourcing of solid waste management to private companies, this problem has persisted and resulted in many side effects on health and environmental hygiene. Some of the factors attributed to outsourcing of solid waste management to private companies include finance, coverage and management of public resources to reduce solid waste management finance budget from local government (Damoah, 2011). Eventhough outsourcing to private companies has helped in extension of coverage areas; the state of the sanitation problems in the metropolitan assembly continues to worsen as population increases in the metropolis especially in the urban slums and busy areas. Numerous policies, environmental conditions and guidelines have also been put in place to ensure healthy living and refreshing environment free of dirt yet scenes displayed on televisions and other sites are abhorable which portrays the country in a bad status in terms of sanitation.

In the Kumasi Metropolis, all residential and non-residential areas are subject to the payment of waste collection fees even in cases where waste is not taken from the individual households but are sent to a centralised place of collection for collective management. The slums and busy areas are particularly characterised by inappropriate waste management issues and their surroundings are mostly filthy and unhygienic as compared to other places of residents. This questions if the people living in and managing these areas pay for waste collection services or the mobilised funds from such areas cannot cater for service delivery. Because some residential and non-residential areas keep solid waste for days before they are collected and disposed-off prior to payments made to waste management companies. It also prompts the question, whether the realities of poor sanitation issues is on the financing of solid waste management.

As the waste stream of the metropolis increases, keeping a clean and healthy environment becomes a burden due to limited logistics, ineffective planning, inadequate supervision and inappropriate demarcation of sanitary sites at catchment areas which need counteract measures put in place to help curb the occurrences of bad sanitation issues and it resultant effects like, flooding and disease (cholera and malaria) outbreak in the metropolis. This situation may be caused by inadequate finances and calls for effective analysis of solid waste management and how it is affected by the financial constraints of solid waste management companies.

1.2 JUSTIFICATION

Low income countries spend a larger percentage (more 60%) of the solid waste budget on collection (World Bank, 2012) and given a very low consideration except in the cities (Ogawa, 2005). This scenario coupled with inadequacy in the local government taxation system has rendered the local government paralysed in finances and provides limited funds to solid waste management sector. Nevertheless, user fees can be supplemented with the local government fund, however, ability to pay service charge is not encouraging in poorer communities of developing countries. Also, clients' unwillingness to pay fees charged makes revenue mobilisation ineffective (Adu-Gyamfi, 2014).

Again Ghana cannot be exempted from countries experiencing issues of financial constraints which have spread through its regions, metropolis and districts including the Kumasi Metropolitan Assembly. According to Damoah (2011), per capita waste generation increases in proportion to increased consumption, tourism and other related activities as economies develop. This results in the growth of solid waste budgetary requirements in municipalities of developing countries which ranges from 20-50% of total municipal recurrent expenditure (MLGRD, 2010). He stipulated that the rise in contracting private sector service delivery in waste management also cause expenditure to rise because capital investment by the private sector is reimbursed through their contract payments. Also payments of sanitary workers' salaries and benefits, fuel and vehicle maintenance expenses, and solid waste budgets are significantly obligated to the Metropolitan Assembly. Aside these, the solid waste budgets may not make provisions for other expenses such as buying spare parts to make repairs, replacing collection bins and purchasing soil to cover waste in landfill (Karki, 2010).

In this situation, solid waste management actors are not able to deliver good quality services due to inefficient operational vehicles and facilities. These circumstances lead to situation which may not help to sustain the appropriate interest and willingness on the part of clients/citizenry to pay for required service delivery. Also the experience of poor and irregular sanitation services by residents often leads to inadequate confidence and mistrust in Local Government operatives. Transplant of foreign technologies to developing countries for waste recycling, recruitment and management of manpower and other resource allocation and mobilisation have also become a big issue for waste management companies. This makes environmental conditions, health and waste management standards difficult to adhere to. Good solid waste service occurs only where reliable, regularized and adequate cash flow is available. Moreover, adequate cash flow enables municipalities to borrow from local financial institutions or banks to supplement periodic revenues and grants provided by central government. Quality service delivery is therefore determined by regularised and adequate cash flow which is supplemented by municipalities borrowing money from financial institutions, resorting to other revenues, grants and central government.

1.3 RESEARCH QUESTIONS

The study is guided by the following research questions:

1. What is the financial contribution of stakeholders to solid waste management in the metropolis?

2. How does finance affect conformity to institutional framework governing Solid Waste Management in the Metropolis?

3. How can potential sources of funds be discovered, accessed, mobilised and managed to finance Solid Waste Management in the Metropolis?

4. What are the current challenges to financing Solid Waste Management in the Metropolis?

5. How can the existing financing mechanisms and resources be sustainably used to manage solid waste in the metropolis to ensure a healthy environment?

1.4 RESEARCH OBJECTIVES

The general objective of the study is to assess the effects of financing on solid waste management on the environmental sanitation in Kumasi Metropolis.

The specific objectives are to

1. Ascertain the financial contribution of stakeholders in solid waste management in the Metropolis.
2. Examine institutional framework governing solid waste management in the metropolis and how its conformity is affected by finance
3. Explore the potential financial resources at the disposal of the waste management institutions in the metropolis
4. Ascertain the challenges of current state of financing in solid waste at the metropolis
5. Analyse how the existing financing mechanisms and resources can be sustainably used to manage solid waste in the metropolis to ensure a healthy environment.

1.5 SCOPE OF WORK

The work was undertaken in the Kumasi Metropolitan Assembly. The metropolis is one of the thirty (30) districts in Ashanti Region, located between latitudes $6^0 35$" and $6^0 40$"N and longitudes $1^0 30$" and $1^0 35$" W and elevated 250 -300 meters above sea level.

The metropolis is a uniting point for vibrant economic activities due to the different kinds of services provided in the healthcare, education, transportation, financial services and commerce to people moving in and out of the metropolis. As a result, waste management processes remains a deafening problem in the metropolis as population and economic activities increases. Even though there are numerous factors that challenge solid waste management, this study seeks to assess effects of financing on solid waste management at the Kumasi metropolis.

1.6 METHODOLOGY

Both quantitative and qualitative research methods were used. A population sample size of Seventy - one (71) respondents were contacted for the study which included some key informants at the Waste Management Department of the assembly, representatives of other private waste management companies, selected market centre users and bus terminal managers. Purposive sampling technique was used in the sampling of the respondents due to the specified nature of information needed for the work. Multiple techniques for the data collection such as in-depth interview and personal observation were also used.

Primary data was solicited with structured questionnaire from heads of market users associations and bus terminal users, management of bus/transit terminal, the head of research of Waste Management Department in the Metropolitan Assembly and coordinators of private waste management companies in the Metropolis.

Secondary data was taken from publications of related study topics and documents on the Metropolitan Assembly.

Research data was analysed using IBM SPSS Statistics 21.0 and the results presented in tables and figures. Qualitative analysis was done by content analysis of feedback of open ended questionnaires.

1.7 LIMITATION

The research encountered the challenges like inadequate information for smooth running of the research due to unwillingness of respondents to answer some questions administered due to discrete and non-discretional reasons. Inadequate time on the part of respondents due to busy schedules delayed the data collection process.

1.8 ORGANISATION OF THE STUDY

This report is organised into five chapters. The first chapter summarises the general context of study; Chapter two acknowledges the relevance of the research literature whiles chapter three explains the study profile and research methodology. Data analysis and research finding were discussed in chapter four whiles the research summary, conclusion and recommendations to issues identified in the study area were outlined in chapter five.

CHAPTER TWO

LITERATURE REVIEW

2.1 INTRODUCTION

This chapter consists of relevant literature of the topic under study. Different research works have been reviewed and used as a basis for the study to compare and contrast the research findings. It also explains the concept of the research putting into consideration key words like finance, management and solid waste in the research topic.

2.2 CONCEPTUALISATION OF KEY WORDS

2.2.1 Finance

Finance describes activities associated with banking, leverage or debt, credit, capital markets, money, and investments. It basically represents money management and the process of acquiring needed funds. It also encompasses the oversight, creation, and study of money, banking, credit, investments, assets, and liabilities that make up financial systems (Kurt, 2019).

Akrani (2011) defines finance as providing necessary funds required by a business entity (companies, firms, individual and others) on terms that are most favourable to achieve their economic objectives. The features of finance may include investment opportunities, profitable opportunities, optimal mix of funds, system of internal controls and future decision making.

Finance, therefore, is the study of investment and the management of money to provide the necessary funds required by an organization on favourable terms to achieve economic objectives.

2.2.2 Waste

Waste can be defined as something which is not useful to the owner and does not fulfil its purpose when its being used (Gourlay, 1992). Waste can be classified into liquid and solid. Other classification is based on the sources, physical properties, composition and risk associated with waste (World Bank, 1999). This is indicated in Table 2.1

Table 2.1 Classification of Waste

Classification	Example of waste types
Generation source	Households, industrial, municipal service
Physical characteristics	Liquid, Solid, Gaseous
Material composition	Organic, Paper, Plastic, Glass, Metal
Risk component	Hazardous and Non-hazardous

Source: World Bank (1999)

As presented in Table 2.1, waste is classified based on the section of society it comes from thus residential, commercial and industrial. It can also be based on its physical characteristics as well as the risk level thus hazardous or non-hazardous. Other classification is the sources of waste (based on activities through which it is generated) and it includes; municipal sources, commerce and industry, agricultural sources amongst others. Composition is another form of waste classification and it includes paper, glass, ceramics and organic waste amongst others as indicated in Table 2.1

Table 2.2 Classification of waste based on physical state of waste substance

Waste type	Examples
Liquid	Sewage Sludge, Bath and Kitchen Waste Water
Solid	Food Residues, Paper, Plastic, Metal
Gaseous	Factory Smoke, Vehicle Exhaust, Burning smoke
Radioactive	Radiation, Uranium, Plutonium, Excess Energy

Source: USEPA (2008)

Hazardous or non-hazardous waste is classified based on the potential health or pollution risk of its materials (US EPA, 2008). Hazardous waste is harmful to health, environment (USEPA, 2008) and requires caution to dispose-off (DELM, 2003). Hazardous waste includes ignitable, corrosives, toxics and acute hazardous waste (US EPA, 2008). Special waste is dangerous to treat, keep and requires special disposal. Special waste includes amputated human parts and contaminated swabs and sharps (USEPA, 2008). Non-hazardous waste however does not pose risk and are easily managed. For example, uncontaminated earth and waste (bricks, sand, gravel etc) (Environmental Council, 2000).

Therefore for the study, waste is something which is no longer useful or fails to fulfil its purpose when being used.

2.2.3 Solid Waste

Different authors have defined solid waste as materials that arise from human and animal activities which are unwanted. According to Zerbock (2003), solid waste includes non-hazardous industrial, commercial, domestic, institutional garbage and construction waste amongst others. It is also defined as neither wastewater discharges nor atmospheric emissions, arising from domestic, commercial, industrial, and institutional activities in an urban area (Ghana Innovation Market Place, 2009).

2.2.3.1 Sources and Types of Solid Waste

Tchobanoglous *et al* (1993) and World Bank (2012) classified solid waste according to the sources and generation facilities, activities and location as presented in Table 2.3.

Table 2.3 Sources and Types of Solid Waste

Source	Waste Generators	Type of Solid Waste
Residential	Single and multifamily dwellings	Food waste, paper, cardboard, plastics textiles, electronic waste among others
Industrial	Light and heavy manufacturing, fabrication, construction sites, power and chemical plants.	Industrial process waste, scraps, off specification products, slag, tailings, Construction and demolition materials, special waste amongst others.
Institutional	Schools, hospitals (non-medical waste), prisons, government building and transit centres	Paper, cardboard, plastics, wood, food wastes, glass, metals amongst others
Commercial	Stores, hotels, restaurants, markets, office buildings	Paper, cardboard, plastics, wood, food waste, glass, metals, special wastes, electronic waste amongst others
Municipal services	Street cleaning, landscaping, parks, beaches, other recreational areas, water and waste water treatment plants	Street sweepings, landscape and tree trimmings, general waste from recreation and tourist sites
Medical waste	Hospitals, nursing homes, clinics	Infectious waste Infectious wastes, hazardous waste, radioactive waste from cancer therapies and pharmaceutical
Agriculture	Crops, orchards, vineyards, diaries, feedlots and farms	Spoiled food wastes, agriculture waste

Source: Tchobanoglous et al. (1993) and World Bank (2012)

They explained the types of solid waste as agriculture waste, food waste, ashes and special waste amongst others. According to them, food wastes are animal, plant or vegetable residues resulting from handling, preparing, cooking and eating food. They also classified waste from households, institutions and commercial activities which can be burnt or not as rubbish. Other types are ashes which are defined as material remaining from burnt wood, coal and other combustible wastes in the environment. Special waste on the other hand include street sweeping, roadside littering, spill over from central containers and debris. Agriculture waste also constitutes residues from agriculture produce which are unwanted and disposed-off. In 2002, World Bank conducted an analysis of household waste and came out with nine main types of solid waste as indicated in Table 2.4.

Table 2.4 World Bank Classification of Solid Waste

Classification of waste	Example of material
Paper	Newspaper, Cardboards, Office papers, other papers
Plastics	Bottles, Expanded polystyrene, Film plastics, other Plastic
Glass	All types of glasses
Metals	Steel cans, Aluminium can, other ferrous
Organics	Organic food, Yard waste, Wood, Textiles, Diapers
Inorganics	Electronic Carpets, Drywall, Other Inorganics

Source: World Bank (2002)

Other classification by the Centre for Environment and Development (2003) is based on origin, characteristics and risk potential of waste. In summary, types of solid waste include, rubbish, agricultural waste, ashes and residues, demolition and construction waste, and clinical waste. Sources include domestic, commercial industrial and healthcare centres.

This research however deals with solid waste management at residential and commercial areas. Also, the World Bank (2002) classification of solid waste was adopted for the study.

2.2.3.2 Components of Solid Waste

Solid waste comprises materials which can be burnt or recycled. Zoomlion Ghana Limited carried out a survey in 2010 which revealed the composition of waste as presented in Table 2.5. While this survey was carried out for Municipal Solid Waste, the composition survey results combined with the total amount of 1200tons of solid waste produced in Kumasi give a good indication of how much of each type of waste material is being produced in the metropolis.

10

Table 2.5 Solid waste composition in Kumasi

Waste Type	Amount of waste	Percentage of Waste
Organic Material	480	40
Inert Material (sand, ash, C&D)	252	21
Plastics	240	20
Paper and Cardboard	84	7
Textiles	84	7
Metals	24	2
Wood	24	2
Glass/Bottles	12	1
Total	1200	100

Source: Nandomah et al (2015)

According to the Table 2.5, organic material forms major part of waste composition followed by sand, ash and C&D and plastics. Whiles wood, glass and metals form the minor components.

2.2.4 Management

Management is often included as a factor of production along with machines, materials and money (BusinessDictionary.com, 2017). According to Drucker (2005), the basic task of management includes both marketing and innovation. It consists of the interlocking functions of creating corporate policy and organizing, planning, controlling, and directing an organization's resources in order to achieve the objectives of that policy (Drucker, 2005).

According to Stuhlman Management Consultants (2009), "Management is the organizational process that includes strategic planning, setting objectives, managing resources, deploying the human and financial assets needed to achieve objectives, and measuring results. Management also includes recording and storing facts and information for later use or for others within the organization. Management functions are not limited to *managers and supervisors*. Every member of the organization has some management and reporting functions as part of their job"(Stuhlman Management Consultants, 2009).

Management is therefore the government of a course of action, through coordinating of efforts and mobilisation of available human, financial, natural and technological resources to accomplish its objectives.

11

2.2.5 Solid Waste Management

According to Tchobanoglous et al. (1993: 7) solid waste management is the control of generation, storage, collection, transfer and transport, processing and disposal of solid waste according to the best principles of public health, economics, engineering, conservation, aesthetics and other environmental considerations and responsive to public attitudes. This implies, an efficient and orderly waste management needs understanding of fundamental aspects and relationships involved. Also, for a sustainable environment, there must be integration of management strategies including source separation, storage, collection, transportation and disposal.

2.3 CONTEMPORARY METHODS OF MANAGING SOLID WASTE

Recently, strategies in solid waste management include source reduction, sanitary landfill, incineration and final disposal (Dennison and Ruston, 1990).

2.3.1 Source Reduction

Source reduction according to Denison and Ruston (1990) is the reduction in volume or harmfulness of solid waste before processing and disposal to landfills. It is the most important factor in waste management which promotes reusable products and packaging (USPS, 2000). It is also an effective way to minimise solid waste generation. With this strategy, wastes discharged from one source may be significant and reused at another setting. The efficiency of source reduction strategy led to a proposition by Tsiboe and Marbel (2004) in Australia, Netherland and Denmark to separate their solid waste for reuse and effective collection to resolve the waste disposal system issues.

Solid waste can be reduced by cutting down the amount of trash one produce by buying recyclable products. Reusing materials multiple times can reduce solid waste examples, refilling a water bottle rather than buying a new one; reusing newsprint as a paper towel; using re-useable cloth napkins instead of paper napkins; reusable cups instead of paper cups; and reusing grocery bags for garbage collection. Again, waste generation can be reduced by reducing the amount of packaging and components of products and buying what is necessary for consumption.

12

2.3.2 Sorting

Asase (2011) defines sorting as the practice of separating post- consumer materials, so that they do not end up in the same waste stream. Source separation of household waste even though practiced, has not been adopted yet in Ghana as part of the solid waste management practice. There are different types of waste separation scheme and these include customary practices (selling post-consumer items to itinerant buyers, exchanging for other items, and giving out as gifts and charity) and collectively organized interventions (obtaining materials for recycling and composting).

Research conducted by Addo (2009) revealed that, 75.3% of the households are ready to separate their waste only if they are given free bins, 72.3% are willing to separate their waste if the waste collection fee will be reduced and 21.9% are willing to separate their waste with no incentive.

Table 2.6. Composition and Volume of Solid Waste Generation in the Kumasi Metropolitan Assembly

Composition	Volume (KG)	Percentage
Organic	1235	19.0
Paper	967	17.5
Plastic	1225	16.5
Glass	562	8.2
Metal	481	8.5
Textiles	403	6.7
Wood	499	10.9
Miscellaneous	799	12.7
Total	6171	100

Source: Kumasi Metropolitan Assembly 2010

The research also found out that sorting of waste for recyclables waste products take place at various levels in waste management process and the first level of plastic waste collection and sorting is done at the households. Thus plastic materials are considered valuable and are used several times before they lose their utility value and considered as waste. This practice is however not on a large scale as many households have still not cultivated the habit of recycling. There are also collectors of plastic waste in KMA and they are grouped into three; street boys, private sector enterprises and scavengers at landfill. Households are however not willing to separate their waste due to inadequate time, inadequate space to accommodate extra bins, perceived health implications, difficulty of separating waste (not knowing the different compositions), perceived high cost and untimely collection by waste management company (Addo, 2009).

2.3.3 Recycling

Recycling is the process by which non-consumable materials are recreated into new products for consumption. Recycling turns waste materials into valuable resources which yield environmental financial and social returns in natural resource and conservation and prevent pollution for economic growth and attractiveness (USEPA, 1999). Recycling can be classified into two types, post-consumer and pre-consumer recycling. Post-consumer recycling involves products recycled after consumption example plastic and glass bottles and newspapers. While pre-consumer recycling involves recycling materials at the production level example rejected bottles which do not fit into production specifications (Tsiboe and Marbel, 2004).

According to Momoh and Oladeye (2010:1), recycling is an efficient strategy for reducing amount of solid wastes that ends up at Landfill and serves as raw materials for industries. According to them, recycling is the best method for solid waste management however it may be cost ineffective due to high cost of technology involved in it as stipulated by Kreith (1994). Henceforth there has been suggestion for adoption of recovery as a waste management technique by United States Environmental Protection Agency (USEPA) (1999).

2.3.4 Incineration

Incineration is a controlled burning process for combustible waste to reduce it to non-combustible (Centre for Environment and Development, 2003: 9). According to Kreith (1994), incinerators have the ability to reduce bulk of waste significantly than any other method and recover useful energy (Steam or Electricity). Incineration kills disease carrying organisms whiles reducing the volume of waste and heat released can be used to generate electricity (Miller, 1999). Kreith (1994) also discovered some factors as major hindrances in utilising the method which include; high degree of technology, and complexity to safe and economical operation to reduce environmental pollution through carbon dioxide emission and high cost of operation.

2.3.5 Final Disposal

In Ghana, solid waste is disposed-off at both legal and illegal dump sites without regards to the adverse effects to the environment (GEPA, 2002). Waste disposal strategies in Ghana Include uncontrolled dumping of refuse, controlled dumping, sanitary land filling, composting, and incineration (Danso, 2011). Table 2.7 shows the percentage distribution of various alternatives of disposing-off waste around the world.

Table 2.7 Distribution of Waste Disposal Alternatives of Various Continents in the World

Continent	Recycling (%)	Sanitary Landfill (%)	Open Dump (%)	Incineration (%)	Open Burning (%)	Others (%)
Africa	3.9	29.3	47.0	1.4	9.2	8.4
Asia	8.5	30.9	50.9	4.7	1.7	4.5
Europe	10.7	27.6	33.0	13.8	11.8	4.4
North America	8.1	91.1	0	0	0	0
Latin America	3.2	60.5	34	2	0	0

Source: UNEP-ISWA (2003)

Solid can be disposed-off in different way however, it must be cost effective and harmless to the environment. Burning, burying and dumping at landfills are ways of disposing off solid waste in Ghana. Table 2.8 shows the refuse disposal methods by households and domestic generators of waste in Ghana. As indicated in the table 2.8, disposal at landfill recorded the highest for both Domestic and Non-domestic waste generators followed by dumping, burning and burying.

Table 2.8 Refuse Disposal Methods by Domestic and Non-Domestic Generators

Disposal Method	Domestic Generator		Non-Domestic Generator	
	Frequency	Percentage	Frequency	Percentage
Burning	19	19	7	23.3
Dumping	26	26	8	26.7
Burying	2	2	0	0
Landfill site	53	53	15	50
Total	100	100	30	100

Source: Addaney and Oppong (2015)

2.3.6 Sanitary Landfill

At the Sanitary landfill, waste is confined, compressed and covered with soil to prevent burning of waste and help recover land for valuable use in Kumasi Metropolis (Center for Environment and Development, 2003). Landfill is the oldest and predominant form

15

of waste management. It was characterised with high level of engineering, planning and administration which differentiate it from dumpsite. Whiles open dumps are characterised by inadequate engineering measures, no leachate management, no gas management and few operational measures, landfills are well organised (Zerbock, 2003)

Kreith (1994: 2.8) stipulated that landfills are one form of waste management that nobody wants but everybody needs. According to him, there are simply no combinations of waste management techniques that do not require landfilling to make the techniques work. Sanitary landfills are constructed in areas where the lands are natural shock absorbers to reduce risks exposer to public health and quality environment. For example construction in an area with clay soil which has tightly packed particles and water resistant and absence of surface water bodies to prevent water contamination (El-Fadel, 1997). In Ghana, there are only two engineered landfills which are located in Tamale and Kumasi (Post and Obirih, 2003). Non-engineered landfills consist of abandoned stone quarries, old mining areas, or manmade holes in the ground at the outskirts of cities and are difficult to access by transport. Although Landfill is considered as an option for waste management, it is expensive to construct, maintain and can cause ground water pollution. The distance to settlement and water body can also be a hindrance.

2.3.7 Composting

Composting is the biological decomposition of organic material under aerobic conditions which is used to recycle organic yard wastes and household food wastes. During the composting process, bacteria and other micro-organisms change organic matter into humus and the process takes one year (Buba, 2013).

According to the UNEP (2009), there are few exceptions to composting which suit the limited resources in developing countries. In composting, microorganisms degrade organic content and aerobic composting converts organic waste to homogeneous humus (Center for Environment and Development, 2003:9). Composting is good technology for waste reduction because of its adaptability to broad range situations and the percentage of organic composition (50%) of solid waste generated (Zerbock, 2003).

2.3.8 Integrated Solid Waste Management (ISWM)

Integrated solid waste management refers to the strategic approach to sustainable management of solid wastes covering all sources and strategies in an integrated manner with emphasis on maximization and efficiency in resource use. There is still a gap to fill in waste management situation even though government and other private entities have made significant efforts to tackle the situation. Prior to challenges in financing waste, a suggestion was made to change waste to recover materials and resource for a significant reduction in final volumes of waste which can be used to generate fund for waste. The 3Rs (reduce, reuse and recycle) forms the basis for Integrated Solid Waste Management (ISWM) system and is approved and received by all local authorities in Wuxi, PR China; Pune, India and Maseru, Lesotho. It indicates appropriate segregation and recycling systems can significantly divert waste from landfills and converted to resources (UNEP, 2009; USEPA, 1999).

2.4 SOLID WASTE MANAGEMENT IN GHANA

2.4.1 Institutions Involved in Sanitation in Ghana

Institutions can be defined as systems of established and prevalent social rules that structure social interactions (Aoki, 2001). At the national level, there are four ministries involved in environment and sanitation. The Ministry of Local Government and Rural Development (MLGRD) and the Ministry of Water Resources Works and Housing (MWRWH) have been the primary ministries involved in policy-making for sanitation and water, respectively. The other two ministries involved in environmental sanitation are the Ministry of Environment, Science and Technology and the Ministry of Health, which handles health data, contributes to policy-making, setting standards, and hygiene education.

2.4.1.1 Ministry of Local Government and Rural Development

MLGRD is the lead agency in the sanitation sector. It is responsible for creating and coordinating sanitation policy, issues guidelines on sanitation services and their management and supervises the National Environmental Sanitation Policy Coordinating Council (MLGRD, 1999). In theory, institutional responsibilities for sanitation are clear, with the Ministry of Local Government and Rural Development (MLGRD) having overall responsibility for formulating environmental sanitation policies.

2.4.1.2 Ministry of Environment, Science and Technology (MEST)

The Ministry of Environment, Science and Technology exist to establish a strong national scientific and technological base for accelerated sustainable development of the country to enhance the quality of life for all. The overall objective of MEST is to ensure accelerated socio-economic development of the nation through formulation of sound policies and regulatory framework to promote the use of appropriate environmentally friendly, scientific and technological practices and techniques and strengthening of application of safe and sound environmental practices.

2.4.1.3 Environmental Protection Agency (EPA)

The Environmental Protection Agency is the leading public body responsible for protecting and improving the environment. It ensures that air, land and water are taken care of by everyone in the society for future generation to inherit a cleaner and healthier world. It ensures environmentally sound and efficient use of both renewable and non-renewable resources to prevent, reduce, and possibly eliminate pollution and actions that lower the quality of life. Also, apply legal processes in a fair and equitable manner to ensure responsible environmental behaviour in the country. According to Vodounhessi (2006), the Environmental Protection Agency is weak because of its high orientation to collaboration. Again enforcement of procedures for sanitation bye-laws should be updated to solve discrepancies and loopholes due preferential treatment, lobbying and outmoded laws (Amoaning, 2006).

2.4.2 Waste Management Regulation and Policy in Ghana

The policy framework guiding management of hazardous solid and radioactive waste include the Local Government Act (490), 1994, Pesticide Control and Management Act (528), 1996, Environmental Assessment Regulations (LI 1652) 1999, Criminal Code Act (29), 1960, Water Resource Commission Act 1999 (LI 1652) and Nation Building Regulations 1996 (LI 1630).

The National Environmental Sanitation Policy (NESP) enacted in 1999 by the Environmental Protection Agency is concerned with sanitation principles, problems, roles and responsibilities of various actors, impact on management and protection, legislation and law enforcement, and criteria for specifying services and programmes, funding, equipment and supplies. A technical guideline "Expanded Sanitary Inspection

18

and Compliance Enforcement (ESICOME)" has being designed from the policy by the MLGRD and implemented by the MMDA's to develop waste management and environmental health plans to solve sanitation issues. This guideline looks at four broad areas namely; Sanitary Inspection, Hygiene Education, Pest/Vector Control and Law Enforcement. Again, the National Environmental Sanitation Policy Co-ordination Council is responsible for policy coordination and ensures effective communication and cooperation between actors of environmental management in respective Districts of Ghana (MLGRD, 2004). There are also standards which include National Environmental Quality Guidelines (1998), Ghana Landfill Guidelines (2002) and Manual for Preparation of District Waste Management Plan in Ghana (2002).

2.4.3 Environmental Bye-Laws in Ghana

According to environmental and sanitation policies all District Assemblies shall promulgate bye-laws addressing

- Establishment of zones for provision of environmental sanitation services.
- Enforcement of public participation in critical environmental sanitation service.
- Designation of areas and facilities for the collection, intermediate storage, treatment and disposal of solid and liquid waste.
- Licensing and monitoring of environmental sanitation services and their collection by contractors, franchisees etc.
- Tariffs for environmental sanitation services and their collection by contractors, franchisees etc.
- Ownership of wastes; Storage of waste on the premises of waste generators; management and disposal of hazardous wastes; individual and communal recycling of waste
- Allowable toilet systems and excreta disposal methods
- The activities and behaviours of individuals and institutions which cause or are likely to cause environmental pollution or vector breeding

These bye laws will be enforced by the Health Inspectorate (Environmental Health and Management Department of the District Assembly) through education and sensitisation. Through this the community will understand and accept its responsibilities with regards to environmental sanitation. However when non-coercive action fails, legal action will be taken through the courts where offenders will be prosecuted at community tribunals.

However, when cases brought before community tribunals cannot be settled, it is forwarded to a higher judicial institution. The police can also be requested to arrest offenders to be brought to justice.

2.4.4 Community Participation in Environmental Sanitation Management

This simply refers to governance and approaches in sanitation management which ensures broader participation in urban environment initiatives for better results in implementation (Menegat, 2002). According to Hueting (1980) and Blaikie and Brookfield (1987), the issues related to environmental degradation are attributed mostly to socio-economic factors. Thus understanding that, factors affecting the community's collective action are crucial to any efforts aimed at championing the people's participation of such resources.

The UNEP (2000) recommends community participation in environmental sanitation problem-solving using the Participatory Hygiene and Sanitation Transformation (PHAST) approach. The PHAST approach encourages local participation in defining problems and solutions related to water, sanitation and disease control by analysing their beliefs and practices then decide what needs to be changed by them. Outside experts, such as local health personnel, water and sanitation engineers and social scientists also participate and share information with community based on principles that, Communities will determine their own priorities for disease prevention and act when they understand the importance of improved sanitation.

A strong commitment on the side of the local government to be inclusive, develop political support, or show leadership will necessitate the involvement of the community as well. This will also ensure acceptance and ownership of government policies and programmes with all residents in the community. It also has to develop and implement the necessary measures to enable various urban stakeholders to perform their tasks and implement their programmes/projects on the environment. Community participation calls for people to participate in planning, implementing and managing their local environment and it means a readiness on the part of both local governments and citizens to accept equal responsibilities and activities in managing their surroundings (UNEP, 2005).

20

2.5 CHALLENGES IN SOLID WASTE MANAGEMENT IN GHANA

Increase in solid waste generation coupled with inadequate disposal and treatment facilities has caused deplorable sanitation issues in the Ghanaian environment since 1990's (Coffie et al 2003). Rapid urbanisation, inadequate funds, bad attitudes, negligence and institutional challenges are all contributing factors (Coffie et al., 2003).

However, a major part of the sanitation issue was attributed to failure of city planners not keeping pace with implication of population growth and financial charges. Though rapid urbanisation is partly a cause of the assemblies' inability to deal with waste issues, the argument is not valid. This is because; development policies continue to discriminate against rural people causing them to migrate to urban centers to access social and economic amenities. According to Research and Development Department office of Kumasi Waste Management Department (KWMD), this situation is inevitable therefore the local governments should expect and make plans towards it. Other challenges include financial inadequacy and limited investment (Dapaah 1989; Adomako 2008).

However, Kendie's (1998) explored the relationship between perceptions, attitudes and beliefs, and sanitation practices which revealed the underlying factors responsible for sanitation issues. He realised that inadequate funding contributed to poor sanitation in the 1970's and 1980's but do not hold due to the steady growth of the Ghana economy. Agbola (1993), Kuako-Asibey and McPherson (1994) also agreed with Kendie (1998) and stipulated the cause of environmental problems can be due to absorbed behavioural patterns and acquired values overlaid on the environment. Therefore an individual whose values do not support good practices is unfriendly to the environment. For example, some people believe children's faeces are not harmful, a woman who has not lost a child should not burry her child's faeces and open defecation is not a problem as cultural practices transcend.

In the developing world a limited part of the urban population is served with solid waste collection scheme (Zurbrugg, 2009). Thus high income people are served at the expense of low income population living in peri-urban areas. Inadequate fees charged and insufficient funds from municipal budget cannot finance services delivered therefore priorities are given to those who can pay. Again, deficiency in institutional management and inappropriate technologies affect sustainability of waste collection services and effective waste management. Finally, negligence of waste management departments in

21

Ghana does not help the situation issues. Until 1990's, water and sanitation sector was neglected and communities' designated institutions had no prioritised Sanitation and Hygienic Practices (Mohammed, 2008; Adomako, 2008). They also discovered the issue of limited institutional collaboration, inappropriate technologies and absence of environmental standards as vital to sanitation factors.

2.6 FINANCING OF SOLID WASTE MANAGEMENT

Financial management and sustainability in waste management from an economic view is a demand driven business, policy driven activity and public good (Scheinberg et al, 2010). It is important in different ways for waste collection, disposal and resource management. Authors have cited scarcity of funds as a major constraint to solid waste management in developing countries (Cointreau, 2001; Ogawa, 2002; Lohse, 2003; Pacione, 2005). According to Lohse (2003:4), fiscal gap widens as urban population expands, increasing demand for infrastructure and services including waste management facilities like central/communal waste bins and vehicles. Lohse explained reasons for municipal finance gap as the absence of independence to establish tax base rate, rate structures and enforcement procedures. Due to this, revenue raised does not correspond with expenditure requirements.

Ogawa (2002) also blamed finance problem in developing countries on inadequacy in development of taxation system of the municipal government level which makes financial base of public services weak. He attributed financial problems to low capacity of local governments for cost recovery and heavy reliance on state subsidies for operations. Attahi (1999) through his work in Abidjan, Cote d'Ivoire found out an elaborate system of taxes and levies such as drainage tax levied on land properties and state subsidies sustain most municipal programmes including waste management. According to his study, only 30% cost of waste management is recovered.

Tagoe et al (2005) also attributed finance problem of governments to inefficiency in financial management and planning among municipal governments. According to the authors, these factors exhaust limited resources available for waste sector and causes unreliable solid waste management services. Again, low priority is given to urban environment and solid waste management in developing countries (Onibokum and Kumuyi, 1999). As a result, the sector's fund provided by national and local government is usually limited leading to unattainable level of service required to protect public health and environment.

Financial difficulty of municipal government can also be attributed to over reliance on central government intervention to provide municipal services (Armah, 1993). According to Armah, any organisation that relies on central government's interventions in operation leads to failure because they are often limited. Therefore, Lohse (2003) suggested internal and external sources of funds from which local governments can raise revenue for financing operations. While some of the sources are being utilised, corruption and inefficiency constrain efforts to raise revenue from other sources (Armah, 1993; Ogawa, 2002).

Again, collection of waste is a public good with a corresponding demand in all cities. It is associated with public health divers and provides strong public and private benefits (Scheinberg et al., 2010) by cleaning cities and protecting public health and environment. Therefore, free riders make the system more expensive by putting pressure on service providers to either enforce fee payment or create incentives for payment. Disposal cost also rises with increasing environmental standards for waste management and investment and operation costs of meeting standards and reducing emissions into the atmosphere.

Again, increased awareness and scientific knowledge of environmental impacts of waste management drive demand for improvement and cost of implementation. However, the risk is mismatched between local needs and external financing priorities which come about through international pressure when local drivers are not strong as in the case of Bamako and Managua with no landfill sites (Scheinberg et al., 2010). In some cases, investment plans are based on internally recognised standards and technologies that may be too expensive or inappropriate for local situations. Investments should therefore be based on local needs, build on existing resources and not put financial burden on users and municipal budgets.

Recycling on the other hand happens for two economic reasons; market value for secondary material and avoiding cost of disposal. This is however confronted by issues such as focus on recycling some type of waste to generate revenue which brings conflict between formal and informal recycling businesses. There is also emphasis on collecting low value materials that raises collection prices without considering the market for recyclables. Some developed countries also struggle with reaching high recycling rates when final elimination options are available at low costs (Scheinberg et al., 2010).

Zurbrugg (2002) maintain fees usually charged for waste collection and insufficient funds from central municipal budgets cannot finance adequate level of service. Again Ahorlu (2006) revealed a major percentage of money for running municipal waste management operations usually comes from limited municipal budgets which calls for efforts to improve overall municipal financial systems. Cointreau (2001) also observed despite the deplorable situation in poor countries, it is common for municipalities to spend 20-50% of available regular budget on solid waste management. This observation agreed with Devas and Korboe (2000) in their study at Kumasi where waste management and sanitation was discovered to be the largest public sector expenditure with logistics alone consuming 45% of regular expenditure. Table 2.9 summarises the solid waste management procedures and cost involved in management practices comparing countries based on their levels of income.

Table 2.9 Comparison of Solid Waste Management Practices and Cost by Income Level of Countries

Classification of countries by income level and activity	Source reduction	Collection	Recycling	Composting	Incineration	Landfilling/Dumping	Cost
Low income	No organised programs, reuse and low per capita waste generation	Irregular and inefficient, limited service to high visibility and wealthy areas	High informal recycling, unregulated imports of materials for recycling example electronic high price fluctuation.	High percentage of organic material, Informal composting, inadequate awareness and market for compost	Not common, unsuccessful due to high capital, technical and operation cost high waste moisture content	Low site technology, open dumping, high land water and environmental pollution, Adverse health impacts on workers and residents	Collection cost represents 80%-90% of municipal solid waste management budget and a small portion allocated to disposal. Fee collection system is inefficient.
Middle income	Practice of source reduction but rarely incorporated into organised program	Increased and improved collection services from residential areas, larger and more mechanised vehicle fleet, collection rates varies between 5080% with transfer stations incorporated.	Informal sector, high technology sorting and processing facilities, relatively high, Imported materials for recycling, regulated recycling rates and considerable price fluctuation	Unsuccessful large composting plants due to contamination and high operation cost, sustainable small scale composting projects, eligible but limited CDM projects, use of anaerobic digestion.	Use incinerators, financial and operational difficulties, less advanced air pollution technology, little or no emission monitoring, finance equipment by subsidies from OECD countries suppliers	Controlled sanitary landfills and environmental effects. Open dump still common, CDM projects for landfill gas are more common	50%-80% cost of budget allotted to collection. More innovation in fee collection example included in utility bills, more mechanised collection fleets and higher disposal expenditure allotment
High income	Organised education programs on ISWM (reduce, reuse, recycle), more producer responsibility and focus on product design	Over 90% collection rate, mechanised vehicles and transfer stations available	High recyclable material collection, sorting and processing services and facilities available and regulated. Increased attention towards long term market for recycled products.	Utilises backyard and large-scale facilities, low compost in waste stream, high source segregation and aerobic digestion and odour control.	Prevalent in areas with high land cost and low availability, presence of environmental control and energy recovery system, emissions are regulated and monitored.	Well engineered sanitary landfills, put into consideration environmental effects and useful reclamation of land value	Less than 10% of budget alloted to collection, large budget allocated to intermediate waste treatment facilities, community participation, reduces cost and increases options available to planners

Source: World Bank (2012)

25

2.7 CONCEPTUAL FRAMEWORK

Literature on the study showed solid waste management as a critical issue in the metropolis. Management is challenged by inadequate funds which form the basis of the study focusing on three key issues namely; solid waste management strategies, actors, enforcement of sanitation laws and the availability of financial resources to cater for all resources used in solid waste management in KMA.

The theory of this study is deduced from the economic context of Schubeler's conceptual framework. It is believed that all efforts of actors in solid waste management are interrelated and relationships and strategies adopted to achieve effective MSWM are directly and indirectly affected by economic factors (finance). The character of waste management tasks and the technical and organisational nature of appropriate solutions depend a great deal on the economic context of the country and/or city in question. The level of economic development is an important determinant of the volume and composition of wastes generated by residential and other users. Also, the effective demand for waste management services, the willingness and ability to pay for a particular level of service is influenced by the economic context of a particular city or area (Schubeler, 1996). The Conceptual Framework for Financing of Solid Waste Management in KMA looks at how to finance solid waste management in the metropolis by harnessing the existing and potential resources in the metropolis available for solid waste management. The goal of this is to provide a clean and healthy environment in the metropolis. The model also talks about the stakeholders in solid waste management of who are the National Government, Local Government (KMA), Private Waste Management Companies (PWMC), Households, Communities and Service users. Even though the adaptation of different strategy by the KMA, which is the involvement of the private sector in the management of solid waste has been helpful, the question still holds to what extent has outsourcing helped to address the solid waste management problems in the metropolis putting into consideration financing as a major factor for outsourcing. Figure 2.1 illustrates conceptual framework of the study.

Figure 2.1 Financing of Solid Waste management in KMA

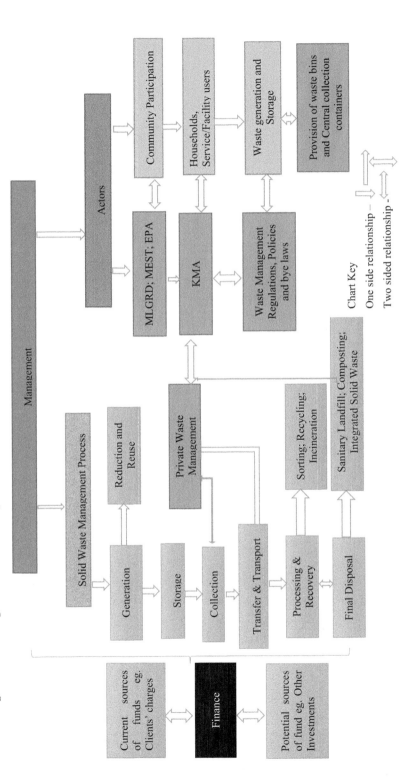

27

The framework shows the linkages between various actors, identifying their functions and how these functions are affected by finance. The conceptual framework as shown in Figure 2.1 explains how the actors in environmental sanitation management; the generators, service providers and the managers come together to solve the issue of solid waste management financially. Generators (comprise households, businesses and government institution) generate waste and use sanitation services; Service providers form the next group of actors and they include private companies and tricycle operators given the mandate to provide sanitation services; and managers constitute the third group of actors (government agencies or departments in the Metropolitan Assembly responsible for planning, organising, staffing, directing and controlling, activities to ensure good environmental sanitation in the metropolis). Managers and service providers are required to render satisfactory sanitation services. When these service providers and managers fail to effectively carry out their responsibilities, it results in poor environmental sanitation condition. On the other hand, when generators do not appropriately dispose-off waste and refuse payment for service delivery, they make the work of managers difficult and promote poor environmental sanitation condition. All these negative activities when left unchecked, lead to deteriorating health conditions of people, increased health cost, environmental pollution and increased cost of providing sanitation services.

Solid waste management displayed at the top of the diagram comprises of two major components namely; Solid waste management process and Actors. The management process includes; waste generation, storage, collection, transfer and transport and final disposal. Whiles the actors include; Ministry of Local Government and Rural

Development, Ministry of Environment, Sanitation and Transport, Environmental Protection Agency, Private waste management companies and the community. These actors however are guided by regulations, policies and bye laws to ensure effective delivery of services to create a healthy living environment through provision and acquisition of solid waste bins and central collection containers at communal sanitary sites. These activities can however be done through a sound financial support system which is indicated at the extreme left of the diagram. It depicts the importance of finance as a contributing factor towards effective and efficient solid waste management in the metropolis.

2.8 CONCLUSION

Despite, the challenges faced in management of solid waste in the metropolis and measures proposed by various researchers, the sanitation issue of the metropolis has not been improved as expected. This may be attributed to inadequate funds for solid waste management logistics, creation of new and mechanised landfill sites and adaptation of modern technology. Financial issues leading to low staff capacity can also cause low collection rate and irregular service delivery in coverage areas which may affect solid waste management services negatively. Again inadequate financial resources can lead to weak institutional structures and poor planning of waste management programmes (Boadi and Kuitunen 2004 and MLGRD 2004).

It is therefore necessary to research into the financing issues of solid waste management of the Kumasi metropolis and discovers possible ways to solve these issues for a better environmental sanitation status. Chapter three explains how this study was done.

CHAPTER THREE

STUDY AREA AND METHODOLOGY

3.1 INTRODUCTION

This chapter gives a summary of the profile of the study area and the methodology used in the study. It further explains the research methods used in collecting data and sampling techniques.

3.2 STUDY AREA

Kumasi, the capital city of Ashanti Region was built from confederacy of states. The metropolis was known as Kumasi City Council in 1995 and it's green environment named it "Garden City of West Africa". It grew outwardly from Adum, Krobo and Bompata in a concentric form to cover an area of approximately 10km radius (GSS, 2011). Currently KMA is the second largest city in the country and its strategic location has endowed with diverse economic and social amenities and services to serve Ghana and other West African Countries. The physical and natural environment has essentially contributed to its social and economic development (GSS, 2011).

3.2.1 Location and Size

Kumasi is located between latitudes 6^035" and 6^040"N and longitudes 1^030" and 1^035"W, elevated 25-300m above sea level. It is approximately 270km north of Accra and share boundaries with Kwabre East and Afigya Kwabre districts to the north, Bosomtwe district to the South, Asokore Mampong and Ejisu-Juaben Municipality to the East and Atwima Kwanwoma and Atwima Nwabiagya districts to the West. It accommodates 36.2% of the region's population and 0.9% of the land area (GSS, 2014). Kumasi is a converging point for brisk economic activities and provides services at various levels in healthcare, education, inter-city transport, financial services, wholesale and retailing amongst others to people.

The metropolis falls within the wet sub-equatorial climate with a minimum temperature of 21.5°C and a maximum 30.7 °C. The favourable climate has a direct effect on population growth as it has caused influx of people from every part of the country.

30

3.2.2 Political Administration

The metropolis was established by Legislative Instrument 1614 (1995) under Local Government Law (1988), NDPC law 207. The Legislative Instrument 1914 amended in 2005 as LI 1805 further divided the Assembly into 10 sub-metros namely Asawase, Asokwa, Bantama, Kwadaso, Manhyia, Nhyiaeso, Oforikrom, Suame, Subin and Tafo. However, Asawase sub-metro was carved out from KMA in 2012 leaving nine sub-metropolitan district councils and political governance in the metropolis.

3.2.3 Transport and Economic Activities

Availability and accessibility to roads help commercial and social activities to thrive in the metropolis. The metropolis has an airport where people commute to Accra, Takoradi and Tamale. About two-thirds of working group in the metropolis are economically active and about nine in every ten of them are employed in different economic activities (GSS, 2011).

The industrial sector employs 38.4% of the workforce in the metropolis and these activities are undertaken at the CBDs; Central market, Adum shopping center, Asafo, Afua Kobi, Bantama, Oforikrom, Krofrom, Tafo, Kwadaso, Atonsu and Suame, Magazines and Sokoban wood village (GSS, 2011). The continuous movement of people in and out of the metropolis for various commercial activities contributes to the solid waste stream of the metropolis especially people engaged in the sales of second hand clothing, shoes, accessories and agricultural produce.

The manufacturing sector employs 13.6% of the population example, food processing, artisans, craftsmanship, furniture and fashion design (GSS, 2012) followed by hospitality sector as the third largest employer in the Metropolis. The manufacturing sector in their bid to convert raw materials into finished products contributes to the solid waste stream even though their management is better as compared to the commercial sector.

Public services are abrupt businesses in the metropolis because of its transit nature while a section of the people focuses on urban agriculture which involves cultivation of vegetables.

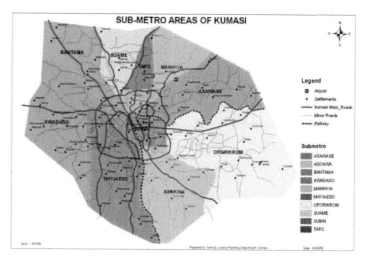

Figure 3.1. A Map of the Kumasi Metropolitan Area

Source: MOFA - KMA, 2009

3.2.4 Population Size and Growth Rates

There has been rapid increase of the Metropolis over the last three decades. The population increased from 1,170,270 in year 2000 to 2,022,919 in 2010 at growth rate of 5.47% pa. This figure represents 42.3% of 4,780,380, the population in Ashanti region. It constituted 47.8% (966,955) males (47.8%) and 52.2% (1,055,964) females with a land area of 214.3km^2 out of the region's 24,389km^2 area and a population density of 9439 persons per km^2 as at 2010 (GSS, 2011).

Overcrowding and pressure on sanitation infrastructure and services, and high rate of waste generation are caused by rapid population growth (GSS, 2011). The continuous increase in population influx into the city contributes to the rate of solid waste generation as the consumption of goods and service increases. Without education and sensitisation on proper solid waste management procedures, the sanitation situation will worsen. Some residents have also built on watercourse which results in flood during rainy seasons. These residents and others at different locations tend to dispose-off garbage into the water bodies and gutters.

3.3 SOLID WASTE GENERATION AND MANAGEMENT IN KUMASI METROPOLIS

According to Mensah and Larbi (2005), Ghana generates 0.45kg per capita average daily waste and about 3.0million tonnes annually. Anomanyo (2004) estimated a daily generation of 1800 tonnes with an average daily per capita waste of 0.5kg in Accra whiles Boateng and Nkrumah (2006) estimated between 1500-1800 tonnes. Averagely, in 2006, 1200 tonnes were collected each day Kumasi. Out of this percentage, private companies collected about 55% (545 tonnes) with the remaining 45% partly recycled/reused, improperly collected and indiscriminately disposed-off within the environment creating environment and health problems (Oduro-Kwarteng et al., 2006). The rate of domestic waste generation was approximately 1000-1500 tonnes a day in the metropolis (KMA, 2010) which was attributed to population growth. As urbanization and population density increases, it becomes difficult for MMDAs to manage quantity of waste generated because people resort to indiscriminate dumping of plastic bags from and fast foods packages in the metropolis.

House-House and Communal Collection are utilised in the Metropolis. However in low income communities where waste collection facilities are limited, communal collection system is used because door to door collection is not feasible (Cointreau levine, 1994). According to Anomanyo (2004), high dependency on agriculture produce for export and consumption in Ghana contributes to the high proportion of food and plant waste. Ketibuah et al (2004) also said the organic volume of household waste in Kumasi is averagely 55% which includes food and putrescible waste.

3.3.1 Solid Waste Collection and Disposal in Kumasi Metropolis

According to Anomanyo (2004), solid waste collection is on franchise and contract basis. Contractors charge fees for frequent collection in high income areas and pay for landfill usage (tipping) fees to the KMA. The communal system however involves collection from public areas which requires the residents to bring refuse to a communal container at a sanitary site for collection by trucks (Cointreau Levine, 1994).

Anomanyo (2004) again revealed that, residence with high population and few collection points always have their containers overflow in many instances. This forces collection site managers to turn away latecomers but in their absence garbage are left to pile up on the ground. Also, collection of waste is planned according to the frequency

33

containers get full and their location. However, collection points have been classified into different types; Type A (daily collection) Type B (Twice in a week collection) and Type C (Once in a week collection) as part of the Nirmal Nagara Programme. Central containers are also used for primary collection in commercial and bulk waste generation areas (Chandra and Linthoingambi, 2009).

Solid waste collected is usually inspected before accepted in to the landfill in Dompoase. The landfill is well engineered with heavy duty equipment which is used for waste spreading. However the facilities are not fully utilised due to inefficiency in functioning.

3.3.2 House to House and Communal Collection Charges

In Assembly's Fee Fixing Resolution, there are two collection service systems. Thus, ¢3 to ¢5 for house to house collection per household per bin per month as operating costs depending on the housing category. The charge was however increased to ¢10 for high-income residential areas whereas middle-income residential areas paid ¢8.00 and low-income class ¢5.00. For communal collection, it was concluded that ¢0.10 to ¢0.30 will be charged per person according to the volume of solid waste being disposed with their own informal standard of measurement (KMA, 2010).

However, before 2008, the communities did not pay any fee for dumping their refuse at the collection or dumping sites because there was no charge for waste disposal at the sanitary sites. Therefore, KMA did not have enough funds to pay the service providers / contractors for effective and efficient service delivery and the collection sites were not well designed. To help mitigate this situation, the City-wide Solid Waste Collection Levy Scheme (pay as you dump scheme), which involves the collection of subsidized user fees from service beneficiaries and clean environmental sanitation status was implemented in 2008 for the two types of services; House to House and Communal Container Collection Systems. With the introduction of the pay-as-you-dump scheme, enough resources were mobilized since the communal collection system was about 80% in localities. These funds have helped improve the collection sites at places like Aboabo and Asawasi. The total cost of waste collection for the year 2011 amounted to ¢3,800,000 ("the annual report of 2011" by KMA-WMD). Out of this cost, service providers were able to recover ¢1,400,000 from the waste charges from house-to-house collection and pay-as-you-dump from the communal sites. The outstanding cost

34

constituted the subsidy to be paid by the KMA (the Central Government) thus ¢2,400,000.

Currently, about 80% of waste collection is undertaken by private organizations. Kumasi Metropolitan Assembly has subcontracted private organizations to assist solid waste management in the Central Business Districts (CBDs). Again, the duty of Waste Management Department is divided amongst the various institutions in the Metropolitan Assembly. The Waste Management Departments oversees the supply of logistics to the private waste management companies for environmental sanitation; Environmental Health Management Department (EHMD) takes charge of public education and inspection of premises. However, sewage systems are in poor conditions, volume of solid waste increase every day and high air pollution. The most affected in the CBDs include; Central market, Roman hill market, Kejetia, Dr. Mensah and Adum. Payment for solid waste collection is however irregular.

3.4 KMA-WASTE MANAGEMENT DEPARTMENT BUDGET

The Waste Management Department (WMD) is an organization within Kumasi Metropolitan Assembly (KMA) structures, entrusted with implementing waste management functions. The WMD is in charge of eight sections of the organisation namely, solid waste management, human waste management, drain maintenance, waste disposal, plant & equipment, public-private partnership contract management, planning Research-M&E, and finance and administration which are all headed by different managers all under the supervision of the waste management manager.

The mission statement of KMA-WMD is to deliver efficient services and embark on programs and environmentally accepted solid waste disposal at affordable cost, collaborating with other actors to keep the metropolis clean and healthy without any adverse impact on the environment to create a healthy environment for living and development".

In the annual budget of the KMA, fund is allocated to waste management from the general revenue sources. Annual budget for the waste management department section from the fiscal year of 2011 was ¢11.18 million or 11.2% of the total annual budget of KMA, consisting of ¢1.35 million for goods and services and ¢9.83 million for fixed capital.

The average monthly service cost of solid waste management services over the years have been paid for by KMA and the Central Government. It costs ¢720,000 covering both collection and disposal which far exceeds the budget of KMA, thus making the assembly to a large extent dependent on central government. The irregular release of funds by the Government often results in accumulated debts to contractors making the service delivery unsustainable. The ten Sub-Metropolitan Areas in the Metropolis are used for solid waste collection zoning by service providers.

3.5 INSTITUTIONS INVOLVED IN SOLID WASTE MANAGEMENT IN KUMASI METROPOLITAN ASSEMBLY

The agencies involved in solid waste management in Kumasi Metropolitan Assembly are the regional office of Environmental Health and Sanitation Directorate (EHSD-MLGRD) and Environmental Health Departments / Units of the surrounding district / municipality. The duty of the Environmental Health and Sanitation Directorate is to monitor, coordinate and evaluate the performance of MMDAs in the region, monitor the use of budgets allocated to the MMDAs, generally review and co-ordinate public services in the metropolis. However, it is confirmed that there are no direct actions by the Regional Office for implementing development programs for solid waste management of the MMDAs. Their main concerns are human resources management and assisting in the preparation of reports by the MMDAs.

3.5.1 Service Providers for Solid Waste Management in KMA

The contractors to provide service for each Sub-Metropolitan Area were selected through the National Competitive Bidding process to provide waste collection services in the ten Sub-Metropolitan Areas after negotiations on the bid prices. The contract period was five years between 2008 and 2012 and was phased; Phase I: January 2008 - March 2009, and Phase II: April 2009 - December 2012.

Table 3.1 Solid Waste Management Service Provider in KMA

Zone No. of Sub-Metros	Sub-Metropolitan Area	Service Provider	Provisional Monthly Contract (¢)
1	Asawase	Osbon Enterprise / Zoomlion Ghana Ltd	33,051.31
2	Asokwa	Sak-M Company Ltd	31,741.67
3	Bantama	Mesh World Company Ltd	33,051.37
4	Kwadaso	Waste Group Company Ltd	37,924.00
5	Manhyia	Mesk World Company Ltd	37,924.00
6	Nhyiaeso	Kumasi Waste Management Ltd	30,733.00
7	Oforikrom	Aryeetey Brothers Company Ltd	37,924.00
8	Suame	Anthoco Company Ltd	33,015.28
9	Subin	Zoomlion Ghana Ltd	37,924.00
10	Tafo	Zoomlion Ghana Ltd	30,051.37
Total			343,340.00

Source: KMA-WMD, 2012

Zoomlion GH Ltd however took over Osbon Enterprise due to problems with the owners of their equipment in an early stage of Phase I. (Phase I: Jan. 2008 - Mar. 2009). Service providers responsible for carrying waste in the KMA submit their reports on their activities to KMA-WMD monthly. The report entails the coverage areas, NYEP (National Youth Employment Programme), state of tricycles, status of sanitary logistics, landscape and beautification, vector control (NAMCOP: National Mosquito Control Programme), human resource issues (personnel status, accidents), challenges, recommendations, and planned activities for the next month.

3.6 RESEARCH METHODOLOGY

3.6.1 Design of Research

Literature on financing of solid waste management and stakeholders involved were reviewed to acknowledge works conducted by other researchers in the field and to emphasize on their success and for smooth conduct of the study. The research design adopted was a case study because the researcher investigated and understood the financial role of stakeholders' involved in solid waste management and the available finances at the disposal of solid waste management companies and operators, challenges of current sources of funds and the sustainability of the available finance mechanism in the Metropolis. This gave a broad view and a deeper understanding of the study within a period of time.

The research strategy adopted was the mixed approach thus utilising both quantitative and qualitative approaches. The mixed method approach was used to achieve a rational correspondence of data because one method cannot wholly capture important structures of the study (Denzin, 1989). Again, the researcher is able to validate the study and make it credible.

3.6.2 Sources of Data

Primary Data

Qualitative and quantitative research methods were used to gather data from respondents utilising interviews, questionnaire and field observation to validate data.

Secondary Data

Journals and published works from researchers were used. Existing documents from Metropolis Waste Management Department and Private Waste Management Companies were obtained to ensure the research outcomes and experiences on the effects of financing solid waste management are logically explained.

3.6.3 Sampling Design

The Metropolis' population is projected to be 2,655,968 people in 2017 using the geometric progression model (Pt = Po*(1+r) ^t) based on the 2012 estimation (2,035,064) according to Ghana Statistical Service, 2012. This indicates a significant increase in the total population of the metropolis within the 5years period which has a direct implication on solid waste generation and management. The research made use of the non-probability method since members of the population were selected in non-random manner for the sake of convenience and some constraints that were expected and chance was given to anyone who was in the position to deliver information through the requirement ensuring that they were within the sampling frame of seventy one (71) people.

Purposive sampling technique was used in the study due to the specified nature of information needed for the work. Whiles multiple instruments were employed for the data collection. It was the intention of the researcher to study many other Metropolis in Ghana due to the problems associated with generalising of findings. However due to financial and time constraints, the Kumasi Metropolitan Assembly (KMA) was chosen for the study which engaged people regardless of their social, economic or political

38

status. The respondents were basically the head of research and development in the Metropolitan Assembly Waste Management Department, Operations managers of private Waste Management Companies, tricycle operators, Bus terminal Managers and Heads of Market associations and users/hawkers. In all a total seventy (71) respondents were contacted and interviewed.

In all, six contracted solid waste management companies were targeted for the study and other tricycle operators where the operations managers were interviewed. The study was undertaken at the 10 sub-metros of the metropolis. Bus terminals and market facilities were selected from these sub-metros and the appropriate questionnaires administered to the respondents. Managers at the bus terminals including private owned and state owned terminals, lorry stations and taxi ranks at busy and less busy areas were interviewed. They include OA Travel and Tour (Asafo Labour), Adehye Bus Terminal (Adehyeman), Cooperative Transport Society (Adehyeman), STC (Adum), Metro Mass Transit (Abrepo Junction), Kwame Antwi Bus Terminal (Rails course), K.O. GPRTU of TUC station (Adehyeman), Kumasi Neoplan Station GPRTU of TUC (Asafo), Imperial Express (Joe Boy Station At Alabar), Dr Mensah (Mampong Taxi Rank, Aboabo and Oforikrom), Tafo bus and taxi Station, Sofoline bus station, GPRTU of TUC (Anloga Junction), Santasi Roundabout taxi rank, Okess Taxi Station (Dr Mensah), Atonsu bus and taxi station, Adum Station (Harper road), Tech, Oduom and Asokore Mampong Station (Tech junction). The motive behind involving both private and state owned bus terminals and taxi ranks at busy and less busy areas were to compare the quality of services delivered by the contracted waste management companies and their respective charges. Also to determine if the location of the bus terminals and the nature of activities undertaken there affect the cleanliness or sanitation situation and to identify the challenges in providing waste management services. These areas served as the major source of finance for solid waste management in the metropolis however, the availability of funds depended on the quality of services provided by contracted solid waste management companies.

Heads of market associations, users and hawkers were also interviewed. The market centers included selected residential markets and central business district market facilities in the metropolis. The residential markets include Tafo Market, Bremang Market, Ayeduase Market, Anloga Market and Atonsu Market. While the commercial markets include Central market, Roman Hill, Adum Market, Suame Market, Bantama

39

Market, Asafo Market and K. O. Adehyeman Market which is a conglomerate of private owned market centers (Acheammfour and Adehye Market). Also grouping of markets to residential and commercial helped to identify the type and nature of services delivered at the various facilities and charges applied to these services. Also to determine whether the level of activities, location and distance of facilities are factors that determines delivery of services and its charges.

3.6.4 Methods of Data Collection

Prior to the administration of the questionnaires, a first-hand survey was made to some of the selected suburbs' market places and bus terminal. Visits were also paid to some public and private busy bus terminals in the metropolis. The Kumasi Metropolitan Assembly Waste Department was also visited to inquire of the best possible help they will be ready to give.

Based on these visits the appropriate people to contact for the administration of questionnaire and interviews were determined for the research work preparation.

Questionnaire Survey

Questionnaire was administered at selected institutions, terminal bus areas and market centers. The questionnaire was pre-coded with both closed and open-ended questions that required the needed information on the topic of research. The questionnaire survey was undertaken and administered to the head of research and development in the Metropolitan Assembly Waste Management Department, Operations managers of private Waste Management Companies, tricycle operators, Bus terminal Managers and Heads of Market associations and users/hawkers. It was segmented to allow efficient gathering of data from the respondents where the issues covered in the survey included: current solid waste management procedures by waste management institutions, financial constraints and other challenges faced by these institutions, existing and potential resources available to be harnessed for solid waste management purpose, effectiveness, affordability and recommendation for improvement in solid waste management services at market centres and bus terminals.

Expert Interviews

Detailed expert interviews were held with staff from various waste management companies; General and Operations managers from the private waste companies and the head of Research department at KMA. Formal and informal interviews and discussions were used to extract important information for the discussion and conclusion parts of the research in addition to the questionnaire. To provide more current data, questionnaire was developed and sent out to Bus terminal managers, Heads of market users, the head of Research department of KMA, the General and Operations managers of Private waste management companies to provide the information needed for successful analysis of this work.

This formed the basis of the primary sources of data where both closed and open ended questions were asked and it aimed to assess the role of finance of solid waste management in Kumasi Metropolitan Assembly. The languages used were English and Twi to enable respondents expresses themselves freely. The mode of discussion was face to face interview and it focused on challenges of solid waste management companies, their sources of funds and other potential resources to be harnessed, and customer satisfaction to delivery of services. The respondents engaged were the Kumasi Metropolitan Assembly Waste Management Department, Private waste management companies and tricycles operators.

Personal observation

Visits were made to suburbs' bus terminals, market and other public places to have an in-depth knowledge and understanding of the research situation. This technique was used to provide vivid and picturesque nature of the sanitation situation in the metropolis. Responses to the questionnaire were used for data evaluation on the delivery of waste management service; alternative methods for consideration; constraints and management strategies.

Administration of questionnaires

After the pre-test, instruments were hand delivered to respondents at various institutions. Some of the questions were closed ended whiles others were open ended. The instruments provided space for the respondents to record their opinion on certain situations. The instruments requested a financial status of the Private waste management companies between a range of possible five (5) years period against which the data were to be recorded and analysed. These instruments centred on the objectives of the study.

3.7 DATA ANALYSIS

Data was analysed using the IBM SPSS Statistics 21.0. From the analysis, discussion was done and conclusions subsequently drawn and inferences made to reflect the purpose and objectives of the study.

Four stages of qualitative data analysis were opened to the researcher for data analysis. These included data assembling from variety of sources, data reduction which involved organization and structuring of qualitative data, data display which involved summary and presentation of the content of qualitative data and finally data verification involving seeking alternative explanations and interpretation of qualitative data.

The following were used to analyse the data for the study; editing of the data to detect and correct, possible errors and omissions that are likely to occur so as to ensure consistency of responses from respondents; coding of the data to enable respondents to be grouped into limited number of categories.

3.7.1 Analytical Framework

Basis for Analysis

Based on the general and specific objectives of the research, data was collected and analysed using the following criteria.

The contribution of various actors in the waste management processes was identified and assessed during the period of study

- Financial contribution of stakeholders was ascertained using the trend flow of finances from various actors into waste management companies.

Analysis was made on adherence and effectiveness of the set up conditions, standards and regulatory framework governing various stake holders in solid waste management in the metropolis putting into consideration time and cost involved. In this the current institutional framework was examined based on

- Procedures involved in conforming to solid waste management standards and regulations and how waste management companies are able to meet them.

42

- Institutions involved in ensuring adherence to regulations and how they operate with solid waste management companies.

- Cost and time factor in conforming to set standards and its effectiveness on solid waste management.

This analysis helped to ascertain cost effectiveness of complete adherence to set up conditions and whether the nature of the conditions promotes conformity by solid waste management service providers. It brought into light how laws are enforced and by who, who is governed by the laws and what punishment is given to law breakers. Lastly, how conformity to laws leads to improvement in sanitation issues.

Analysis was also made on the potential sources of funds. This analysis made use of financial information taken from waste management companies

- Discover potential sources of funds

- Determine the payment schedule for services provided and how companies can factor it into their finance system

- How funds can be retrieved, organised and managed to finance solid waste management in the metropolis was also put into consideration.

- Determine the possible challenges to be encountered in accessing these funds and how to overcome them.

Analysis was also made on the current sources of funds at the disposal of solid waste management companies for financing waste management and challenges they face in accessing these funds for operations in the metropolis. Data collected was used to:

- Determine the current sources of fund available to waste management companies

- Determine how the funds are allotted and used by waste management companies in their operations

- Determine the challenges faced in accessing, allotting and use of funds within and outside the company and how possible they can be solved

- Assess the satisfaction in delivering services and readiness of clients to pay amount charged. In this, responses from service utilisers (bus terminal

43

managers and heads of market users) were stroke against the responses of waste management service providers (KMA, private waste management companies).

How the existing sources of funds can be sustainably used was also be put into consideration. This analysis made use of financial data from solid waste management institutions.

- Determine how effective and helpful the existing sources of funds have contributed to solid waste management in the metropolis

- Determine how possible they can be utilised without exhausting or abusing the source of fund flow.

- Also identify the current and future prospects in these sources of funds for solid waste management.

3.8 CONCLUSION

As population size increases in the metropolis, the rate of economic, commercial and social services and activities also increases to meet the demands of the people. These activities directly and indirectly contribute to the waste stream of the metropolis especially in the commercial areas likes CBDs, markets and bus terminals. The role of the major stakeholders in solid waste management in the metropolis in keeping in environment clean and healthy has been encouraging in the past years and there is more room for improvement.

However, challenges like financing has been one of the major factors in delivering solid waste management services by waste management companies and the case study design adopted to research into the financial status of solid waste management companies, how their finances affect service delivery and the appropriate counteract measures to be adopted to solve these challenges gave some significant data for analysis. This analysis is captured in chapter four and explains the research data extracted from respondents on financing of solid waste management and its effects in the sanitation situation of the metropolis.

CHAPTER FOUR

INTERPRETATION OF DATA, ANALYSIS AND DISCUSSION

4.1 INTRODUCTION

This chapter explains data collected from selected sample frame of the research work by use of charts and tables and comparison with existing literature reviewed to bring out concrete evidence in support or in contrast with findings of the study.

4.2 ASCERTAINING FINANCIAL CONTRIBUTION OF STAKEHOLDERS IN SOLID WASTE MANAGEMENT IN THE METROPOLIS

4.2.1 Bio Statistical Data of Respondents

The study conducted targeted a total population of 71 respondents. Forty respondents from the market centers, 20 respondents from bus terminals, 10 respondents from private waste management companies and one respondent from Kumasi Metropolitan Assembly. The information from the respondents served as the basis for quantitative and qualitative analysis of the study and helped in achieving the general and specific objectives. Out of the 70 respondents, respondents from the market centers and bus terminals amounted to 60 people with 26 of them being males and the remaining 34 females. The remaining 10 respondents from the private waste management companies were males whiles the representative for KMA was a female. This indicates a higher representation of females in solid waste management in residential and non-residential areas. However, the male respondents dominated in the management solid waste in bus terminals and private waste management companies whiles the females represented the market centers. This shows that the role of males in solid waste management is more formal as compared to the females. Information from respondents was to inform the study the roles they perform in solid waste management in terms of finance and for them to validate information given by other stakeholders.

Table 4.1 Gender of respondent (Market centers and bus terminals)

Gender	Frequency	Percentage (%)
Male	26	43
Female	34	57
Total	60	100

Source: Field Survey, 2017

Twelve percent of the respondents were tertiary school leavers while 47% were Junior high school graduates, 10% had no formal education and 27% were 0-level graduates as presented in Table 4.2. This indicates a high rate of literacy in the sector of the economy. This response was no different from the educational level of the respondents from the private waste management companies because 8 out of the 10 respondents were literates with 4 being masters' degree holders and the remaining 4 senior high school graduates. This also implies that solid waste management is not affected by illiteracy

Table 4.2 Level of education of respondents (Market centres and bus terminals)

Level of Education	Frequency	Percentage (%)
No formal Education	6	10
Elementary/Primary School	3	5
Junior Sec/Middle school	28	46.7
Senior Sec./O-Level	16	26.7
Tertiary	7	11.7
Total	60	100

Source: Field Survey, 2017

4.2.2 Profile of Private Waste Management Companies in KMA

Four out of the six contracted waste management companies in the metropolis helped in the study and 6 tricycle operators were randomly selected. According to these contracted companies, it is prudent for the KMA to outsource refuse collection because the local government cannot handle generated waste by the locality and outsourcing make it less burden for KMA in solid waste management. Also, the KMA does not have adequate resources to manage all the waste within the metropolis because waste management is highly capital intensive. Therefore, engaging external vendors to aid in refuse collection in the metropolis can be sustained if clients pay the exact amount they are charged without any interference by government. Again, division of labour leads to efficiency however; KMA has inadequate funds and logistics to manage solid waste in the metropolis. The private tricycle system can also help out but it is not feasible as compared to the companies because their operation is not frequently regulated and they serve a small portion of the metropolis.

Tricycle Operator 1 (Mc-Iliase De Christ)

The operations of this tricycle operator covers Buokrom Estate and operates with only one tricycle and charges between ¢1 -¢20 depending on the quantity of the waste and customers are free to bargain the price. The general operation of the tricycle amounts to ¢928 every month which entails fuel cost, servicing of tricycle and disposing cost at landfill site thus he spends ¢30 per day and an extra ¢7 on every weekend for maintenance. Fuel costs ¢15 each day throughout the month (¢450 per month) and disposing fee is also ¢15 per day.

Plastic bags and food waste dominates the waste normally collected while solid waste is stored by clients in dustbins and sack bags. The company is engaged in house to house collection and uses tricycle to dispose solid waste off at the landfill. The distance between his coverage area and disposal site is approximately 26km which affects the cost of transportation cost and duration for disposal. His operations are guided by the KMA's byelaws but they are not enforceable. Some of the issues brought out my the operator concerning his operations include;

Tricycle operator 1 "I have been asked not to use waste tricycle to collect foodstuffs or any other items".

Tricycle operator 1 "The people are stingy and don't want to pay for the collection fee, it makes the environment unclean..... The people should therefore be sanctioned and it will make them pay for the amount charged for waste collection".

Tricycle operator 1 "I recommend that the streets in the coverage area should be improved upon to promote effective waste collection. More landfill sites should be constructed and properly maintained..."

Plate 4.1 Tricycle for Operator 1   **Plate 4.2 Tricycle for Operator 2**
Source: Field survey, 2017

Tricycle Operator 2

The coverage area is Tech, Boadi and surroundings. It utilises house to house and bus terminal collection with one tricycle and charge ¢1-¢3 of waste from household and as high as ¢20 depending on the quantity of waste at bus terminals. However, clients are not willing to pay the charges so they bargain. The company spends between ¢27 and ¢32 per day thus ¢885 per month on fuel, tricycle servicing and washing. He also raised issues about the flexibility and relevance of their operation stating that *"It is very sustainable to engage tricycle in solid waste management because we are not governed by any rules; we just have to register and pay ticket"*.

Tricycle Operator 3

Operates within Boadi and Ayeduase doing household and hostel collection and normally charge between 70 pesewas to ¢3 based on the quantity of waste however, clients are not willing to pay so they always bargain. Daily expenditure on operation amounts to ¢80 per day thus ¢2400 per month on fuel, servicing of tricycle, washing and sales payment to the owner of the tricycle. The association of tricycle operators organise labour once in a month to embark on a free clean up exercise in the coverage area as part of their community service to the society. This tricycle operator is environmentally conscious and abides by some rules. He stated *"I cover the waste with net during transfer and transportation. To help improve the collection system, KMA should help sensitize and punish the people for keeping dirty environment"*.

Despite the efforts of the tricycle operators, challenges like delays in disposing off waste at the dump site (Sokoban wood village) due to long queues is unavoidable and they always have to pay their way through aside the official charges. Again the challenge of the people refusing to pay their charges makes solid waste collection difficult. Also the disposal fee at the landfill site has been increased from ¢3 to ¢15 but clients are not willing to pay the current price charged for waste collection. Their profit margin is low as they have to spend most of the revenue on their operating expenditure leaving a little amount for personal and family upkeep. Some are therefore forced to use their tricycle for other menial jobs like load carriage in central market after waste disposal eventhough that is not acceptable by the KMA because it is unhygienic, stinky and poses health issues. Others are also engaged in other economic activities while those who don't engage in any other activities depend on the remaining meagre amount for survival till the next day's work.

Kumasi Waste Management Limited

The coverage area of Kumasi Waste Management Limited is Nhyiaeso sub metro and collection is done mostly in the morning. Kumasi Waste Management Limited also undertakes liquid waste collection and utilises house to house and communal collection using transfer sites. The collection vehicles go to 50-100 houses before it gets full whiles above 250 houses contributes to the central waste collection containers. Currently, the company operates with six vehicles, some compactors, roll-on-roll-off, multi lift and bola taxis. Household collection is done once in a week and vehicles (two compactors, Roll on – Roll off) go to the landfill site twice a day as and when they get full. The Assembly sets charging rate for waste collection for the sake of cost uniformity and affordability by clients. Private waste companies pay ¢30 per tonnage of waste collected for disposal instead of ¢60. This cost is however imposed on the clients as they access their services and those who dump at the communal sites pay ¢1 per head. Clients are provided with 240 litter bins at a fee and it costs ¢350 at market price. These bins are sold to household because in the contract with KMA, the households are supposed to provide their own bins. The company spend ¢80,000 on fuel, spare parts, vehicle servicing, salaries, PPE's etc every month.

Zoomlion Ghana Limited

The coverage areas for operation are Tafo and Subin Sub-metros and collection is done throughout the day from morning to evening. Zoomlion Ghana Limited is also engaged in liquid waste collection, clinical/medical waste collection, recycling, composting and conversion of waste to energy.

The company make use of household and communal collection using sanitary sites which cover about 200 to above 250 houses before collection vehicles becomes full and disposes off at landfill site. The number of houses however varies depending on the capacity of the vehicle. However 13 vehicles are used for operations in the catchment areas in KMA. There are other forms of transport used by the company which include motorised tricycles and the three wheeler vehicles. The average cost of solid waste transfer from various collection points by the company to the landfill is ¢7000 per day. The company has no disposal site and therefore uses the Oti / Dompoase landfill site.

The average distance from all collection point in the metropolis to disposal site is 15 km. This does not determine cost of transportation and disposal however there is payment of fees for solid waste disposal. The fee at the disposal site ranges between ¢40 and ¢70 depending on the tonnage of wastes disposed by each vehicle. KMA has fee fixing for contractors therefore the company uses KMA's standard for all charges. Customers however remain indifferent with the solid waste collection charges. 50 designated sanitation sites are under the company's catchment which is mostly cached from the sub-metro's development plan.

There is also provision of 240liter bins for clients at an average cost of ¢250 and the number of bins requested by a client depends on the waste generation rate of the client. The household collection rate charged depends on the frequency of solid waste collection and amount of waste collected from each household. The average price is ¢25 per month. Whiles the communal collection rate charged depends on the quantity of solid waste disposed-off by individuals at the sanitary site.

SAK-M Company Limited

Aside waste collection, the company undertake office cleaning services. It operates within the Asokwa sub-metro and waste collection is done in the mornings, afternoons and evenings. Averagely, 480 tonnes of Solid waste is collected in a day thus 14,400 tonnes a month. House-house and industrial waste collection system is utilised with the company conveying 12% of total solid waste in the metropolis to landfill.

The vehicles cover 50-150 houses before it gets full and sometimes depend on the type of waste being collected. Whiles above 250 houses contribute waste to the central waste collection containers. Recently, the company has 5 vehicles used for operations and provides waste bins to clients thus 1 bin to each household at a cost range between ¢200 and ¢250. However, for the waste collection system to be improved, operational areas should be sub divided and assigned to good supervisors for proper monitoring. The charges for house to house collection ranges between ¢15 and ¢30 based on the quantity of waste collected and the frequency of collection whiles communal collection rate depends on the volume of waste. This standard of charging has been approved by KMA and willingness of costumers to pay charges depends on the quality of service. Even though increment in rate will be appreciated by the company; there must be approval from the assembly. The company spends approximately ¢35,000 on fuel, spare parts, servicing of vehicles, container maintenance and administrative cost every month.

Asadu Royal Seed and Waste Management Limited

The company's coverage areas are Oforikrom and Manhyia sub-metro which includes 17 areas. Waste is collected any time in the day and sometimes clean up exercises are organised in these areas. In all the company collects about 200-250 of 240 litre bins of solid waste in a day thus 3 compactor vehicles and 35 tipper bins. The modes of collection of waste are house to house collection and communal collection using sanitary sites. Currently, about 2500 houses enjoy the company's services every day and based on the amount of waste generated by households, between 150-200 houses can make one vehicle full and sometimes above 250 vehicles. Also 100-150 houses contribute to the central waste collection containers at some places and in other places above 250 houses.

The company uses three vehicles for operation and other vehicles such as skip trucks for central waste bins. Clients are also provided with 120 or 240 litre bins for solid waste storage in the households. However, the number and size of waste bins given out to clients depends on the volume of waste generated. The 120 litre bin costs 150cedis whiles the 240 liter bin costs ¢200. Wastes are collected from houses on a daily or weekly basis whiles sanitary sites waste are collected when the containers get full. The vehicles also collect waste to the landfill site once or twice in a day and the charge for waste collected always depend on the quantity of waste. The company charges between ¢20 and ¢40 cedis for household collection and ¢0.50 pesewas upward for household communal collection. However the clients are not willing to pay these charges because they don't see the need to pay for it which makes it difficult to increase the charges. Currently, the company has 35 sanitary sites within their catchment areas and the KMA does the designation of sanitary sites. The distance from collection sites to landfill somehow determines the cost of transporting waste and the company spends ¢9,600 on transportation and disposal every month. In general the company spends ¢45,000 every month on fuel, spare parts, servicing of vehicles etc.

4.2.3 Service terms of Private waste management companies in KMA

Four out of the 10 waste management companies interviewed were well established and contracted by KMA to undertake solid waste collection while the remaining 6 were operating informally with tricycles. Two out of the four contracted companies have worked with KMA Waste Management Department for more than 15years, whiles 1 has worked with KMA Waste Management Department for between 10 years and the remaining one for 5years as indicated in Table 4.3.

Table 4.3 Number of years in contract with KMA by Private waste management companies

Variable	Frequency	Percentage (%)
5-9	1	10
10-14	1	10
More than 15	2	20
Less than 5 years (Tricycle operators)	6	60
Total	10	100

Source: Field Survey, 2017

Even though the KMA has contractual agreement with both tricycle operators and private waste management companies almost all the tricycle operators do not abide by the solid waste management contract terms and conditions of the KMA because, they operate on their own as informal contractors and are not bound by any conditions except payment of disposal fees. Some of the contract terms include avoiding the use of tricycles for other economic activities (carriage of food stuffs and other edible items in the commercial areas) after disposing off the garbage collected from clients. These economic activities serve as a second source of income to tricycle operators for covering maintenance and operations fuel cost.

Also, two of the formally contracted private waste companies are struggling to meet the operational terms due to financial constraints. Some of the terms include proper and frequent maintenance of collection vehicles and central waste bins. Funds mobilised from clients who use the central waste collection systems are not adequate to provide new central waste bins and maintain old ones.

Table 4.4 Companies ability to meet KMA contract terms on solid waste management

Variables	Frequency	Percentage (%)
Yes	2	20
No	7	70
Maybe	1	10
Total	10	100

Source: Field Survey, 2017

The responsibility of the KMA is to provide private waste management companies with logistics like vehicles and waste bins to make their work effective in the metropolis however they are not obliged to give the private waste management any financial support. Even though the Kumasi Metropolitan Assembly provides logistics to the solid waste management companies, it has been an issue due to inadequate finance. The feedback from respondents indicates nine out of ten disagreeing financial support from the KMA.

Table 4.5 Financial obligations of KMA to Solid Waste Management Companies

Variables	Frequency	Percentage (%)
Yes	1	10
No	3	30
Not Applicable	6	60
Total	10	100

Source: Field Survey, 2017

Currently there are nine sub metros in the metropolis and these sub metros' solid waste is being managed by six private waste management companies. There have been some changes in the private waste management companies in the metropolis since some of the previous companies' contracts have phased out and new ones have been factored in the solid waste management processes. The new companies and their coverage areas are listed in Table 4.6

Even though these companies have been assigned to the various sub metros, Zoomlion Ghana limited mostly sweep the general streets, roads, public places and CBDs with the support of the Kumasi Waste Management Limited in the solid waste collection. The remaining companies are however engaged in only house to house and communal collection of households and market places found within their catchment areas based on contract terms. Tricycle operators also deliver their services in these areas as independent service providers serving as back-ups for the contracted companies.

53

Table 4.6 Service providers and their catchment areas

Zone No. of Sub-Metros	Sub-Metropolitan Area	Service Provider
1	Asokwa	SAK-M Company Ltd
2	Bantama	Kumasi waste management Ltd
3	Kwadaso	Vellmark
4	Manhyia	Asadu Royal Seed and waste Company Ltd
5	Nhyiaeso	Kumasi Waste management Limited
6	Oforikrom	Asadu Royal Seed and waste Company Ltd
7	Suame	Anthoco Company Ltd
8	Subin	Zoomlion Ghana Limited
9	Tafo	Zoomlion Ghana Limited

Source: Field Survey (2018)

4.2.4 Solid Waste Management Processes

According to Kumasi Waste Management Limited, the sources of solid waste in the metropolis includes schools, corporate institutions, market places, households etc and 64-65 % of the solid waste are organic. The sanitary sites are designated to accommodate waste from the public and it is done by the assembly. One container is placed at each sanitary site except areas with high rate of solid waste generation example Aboabo station. Activities like loading, raking to heap or spread the waste in the container and collection fees are undertaken at the sanitary sites. Some of the collection containers are protected from the weather and are emptied when they get full to the landfill site. Between 1000 -1500 tonnes of waste are collected daily to the landfill site because all the companies except Zoomlion Ghana Limited have no recycling unit. Solid waste can however be used by incinerating to generate energy. The private waste management companies have no landfill site and therefore dispose-off waste at Dompoase landfill site owned by the KMA. Also the average distance between collection points to the disposal site is between 10 – 20 km and this determines the cost of transportation. The average total monthly cost of transportation and disposal of solid waste by companies is between ¢30,000 and ¢40,000 per month.

For recycling to be effective, there should be source separation of waste. Thus, a client must have more than one bin to separate waste into organics, plastics, papers, etc to improve the value chain of waste. Companies are willing to give incentives to customers for source separation and the incentive will be based on management decision. For example, provision of free bin per client where the total estimate will be ¢250 multiplied by the number of clients and number of bins needed by each client.

Solid waste can be reused through recycling for farming and manufacturing of other plastic items. They can be remoulded into 240litre bins whiles others can be converted to energy and compost.

According to the operations manager at the Kumasi Waste Management Limited

"The companies have no landfill site; therefore dispose solid waste at Dompoase landfill site. The distance between the collection point and the disposal site however depends on where the solid waste is picked from eve though the distance may affect cost of transportation and disposal to the company; it is indirect because KMA factor it into their fee fixing. A fee is also paid at the disposal site and the charge depends on the volume of solid waste for disposal".

Again, *"Source separation of waste can be helpful but not encouraged at the collection level because it is very expensive to operate. At source separation incentives to be given to clients will be decided by the top management however, clients who engage in sorting will be provided with polythene bags"* as stated by operations manager at Asadu Royal Seed and Waste management.

Waste generation in the metropolis is proportional to population growth which implies that waste will always be generated as population increases. The current process for solid waste management used in the metropolis include, storage, collection, transport, treatment and disposal but solid waste treatment is done by only Zoomlion Ghana Limited. Some recovery and processing strategies used by the company include; plastic recovery and processing into litre bins and bin liners.

Solid waste is stored in 240 litre bins at the household level and in communal containers at the sanitary site for collection. Table 4.7 illustrates the type of storage containers for solid waste in the metropolis. These wastes are collected using compaction trucks and skips as well as roll on/off and disposed-off at the landfill. Sorting of waste is done at the container sites and landfills by attendants and scavengers. However, sorting has its associated costs because a client needs more than a bin to do so. According to the KMA Waste Management Department 5%-10% of solid waste is recycled in the KMA and the remaining 95%-90% is sent to the landfill as at the time of the study.

Table 4.7 Storage containers of facility users in the metropolis

Storage Container	Frequency	Percentage (%)
Basket	1	2
Polythene bags	10	17
Plastic dustbin	11	18
Zoomlion containers	12	20
Wooden box	2	3
Others	24	40
Total	60	100

Source: Field Survey, 2017

From the study it was revealed that 40% of the respondents store solid waste in the open space at both the market and bus terminals for collection especially in the market centres. Bus terminals especially the busy ones in the central business district have no better system of storage f solid waste while the private and state owned ones like the STC, OA and Metro Mass Transit can boast of a good storage system. Zoomlion containers can mostly be found in well organised bus terminals and market facilities whiles plastic bags are mostly used by some market facility users and few taxi ranks. The high rate of open space storage indicates inadequate central or small collection waste bins in these areas to solid waste collection which is as a result of inadequate funding for the provision of such logistics by solid waste management companies and the Kumasi Metropolitan Assembly Waste Management Department.

Plate 4.3 Households storage bin

Source: Field survey, 2017   **Plate 4.4 Recycled storage bin (market)**

Plate 4.5 Storage bin at market centre

Source: Field survey, 2017

Plate 4.6 Storage in sack bags

Plate 4.7 Open dumping on market streets

Source: Field survey, 2017

Plate 4.8 Open dump in gutter at market center

Plate 4.9 Open dump at bus terminals

Source: Field Survey, 2017

Plate 4.10 Open dump, storage in sacks and basket

The facility users do not see the need to sort waste out because most of the people do not have time whiles others do not see it's importance even though they are aware of the benefits of sorting and recycling as indicated in Table 4.8. In the study, 47% of the respondents said they have no time to sort out solid waste whiles 38% of the respondents said it is not important to sort out solid waste. However there are some people around who pick up sachet water rubbers, frozen chicken boxes, provision and confectionary boxes and other box containers for sale and or reuse. Plate 4.11 shows some sachet plastics collected for recycling. Some of the rubber waste is recycled into solid waste bins. The study also revealed that 62% of the respondents have knowledge about recycling and its importance whiles the remaining 38% have no idea about it. The high knowledge of the relevance of waste segregation and recycling can serve as an advantage for solid waste management companies to develop this potential source of funds by paying people for segregation for recycling purposes for an effective solid waste management and business development.

Table 4.8 Sorting of solid waste before Disposal

Response	Frequency	Percentage (%)
Yes	8	13
No	52	87
Total	60	100

Source: Field Survey, 2017

Plate 4:11 Sorting of Plastic (Sachet water packs)
Source: Field survey, 2017

58

Even though the time for solid waste disposal may vary from one facility to the other, the facilities mostly dispose- off solid waste in the mornings (bus terminals and taxi ranks outside CBD's) while the busy bus terminals and market centers dispose-off in the evenings. Dumping of refuse is however done by contracted solid waste collectors or companies to the landfill site in Sokoban wood village. Most of the market facilities have no waste bins placed at advantage points unless in the evenings where clean up and solid waste collection is done for disposal. Market users therefore resort to open space dumping at their trading place. However sometimes, these containers are abandoned in the facilities for an overdue time that they overflow and scatter around the facilities creating unhygienic scenes.

Plate 4.12 Abandoned Storage
containers at Dr. Mensah

Plate 4.13 Abandoned Storage
container at Bantama Market

Source: Field Survey, 2017

Tchobanoglous et al (1993), key elements in solid waste management which include: waste generation, storage, collection, transfer and transport, processing and recovery and final disposal came into agreement with the study's findings as there is first storage in either dustbins or skips for generated household and communal waste which is then collected and finally disposed-off in landfill. Again, collected waste was transferred from small collection equipment like the tricycle to a bigger truck for final disposal.

Waste generation rate per person in the metropolis according to the study amounted to 0.5% per person. Whiles the daily generation rates available for some selected cities and regions, are approximately 0.5 kilograms per person per day and in some cases reaching as high as 0.8 kilograms per person per day (Environmental Guidelines for Small-Scale Activities in Africa, 2009). The study also confirmed the collection of 1200 tons of solid waste generated daily by the metropolis as revealed by the Kumasi Metropolitan Assembly (2006) "the domestic waste generation in Kumasi was approximately between 1000-1500 tonnes a day which was attributed to population growth". There is also a rapidly increasing rate of waste generation over the years as stipulated by Martin (2011).

Storage of solid waste in market centres are mostly done open space except in few organised places where they are kept in waste bins. Waste collection is mostly done by contracted labour and tricycle operators. Even though private waste management companies are doing their best to meet the expectations in delivery of better services to the public, most times they are not able to meet these expectations because public waste containers are left unattended to for some days causing dirty and unhealthy scenes especially in the rainy season. Also vehicles used for the transportation of waste are covered as suggested by the Ministry of Environment and Forestry Notification in Delhi (2000). However, most of the tricycle operators do not cover their trucks.

Only one company (Zoomlion Ghana Limited) is engaged in processing and recovery of solid waste in Ghana which is not significantly recognised. There are also solid waste (sachet water rubbers) pickers involved in small and medium scale recovery and reuse operation as stipulated by Palczynski (2002). Plastic materials are considered valuable and are used several times before they lose their utility value and considered as waste. The collectors of plastic wastes in KMA are mostly women and private sector enterprises. Households are however not willing to separate their waste due to : inadequate time to separate, inadequate space to accommodate extra bins, perceived health implications, difficulty of separating waste (not knowing the different compositions), perceived high cost with separating at source and untimely collection by the waste management company as discovered by Addo (2009).

Open space dumping is common in busy bus terminals and market centres. This is attributed to absence of waste bins in these areas however, in some instances where waste bins are placed at advantage points, the users still litter around because they may be far away from the waste bins or do not see the essence of keeping a clean environment. This confirmed the study in Ado-Akiti, Nigeria by Momoh and Oladebeye (2010). However, Momoh and Oladebeye's (2010), assessment of waste situation in Ado-Akiti did not explain what brought about the indiscriminate dumping.

60

The study also revealed some solid waste disposal major concern and direct issues such as indiscriminate dumping, inadequate disposal sites, issues with proper solid waste disposal due to deterioration of road ways, escalating traffic woes and no substitute for transportation as postulated by Web Governments (2011). In Ghana, solid waste is ultimately disposed-off in both authorized and unauthorized waste dumps without regards to the adverse effects on the environment (Ghana Landfill Guidelines Environmental Protection Agency, 2002). The methods for solid waste disposal in Ghana include; uncontrolled dumping of refuse, controlled dumping, sanitary land filling, composting, and incineration (Danso, 2011). However, there is no incineration and composting of solid waste therefore a higher percentage of solid waste is sent to the landfill site after collection.

4.2.5 Actors in Financing Solid Waste Management

According to the head of research and development at KMA waste management department, local government is in charge of keeping the metropolis clean. The KMA has been in solid waste management services for about 14 years now and they see poor sanitation in the metropolis as a result of the people's attitude and inadequate financial resources to manage solid waste. Currently, the approach used by KMA in waste management is generation, collection and disposal to the landfill site which involves the generators, private sector in waste management and waste management department in the metropolis. However the approach to waste management is not good enough due to inadequate financial support for the waste management department.

Kumasi Metropolitan Assembly Waste Department is in charge of waste management at the Central Business Districts (CBD) in the metropolis. These places include; Adum proper, Dr. Mensah, Central market, Alabar, Roman hill, Bantama, and Suame roundabout which have been outsourced to various private waste management companies in charge of the sub-metros and clean-up is usually done during the night. The assembly also utilises house to house and communal collection which is also undertaken by the private waste management companies (Asadu Royal Seed and Waste Management Company, SAK-M, Anthoco, Vellmark, Zoomlion Ghana Limited, Kumasi Waste Management Limited and Tricycle operators).

According to the Waste Management Department, the assembly collects over 1200 tonnes of solid waste per day and spends ¢60 per tonne on both collection and disposal.

However, solid waste service beneficiaries pay 50% of the cost (¢30 out of the ¢60) for waste collection and disposal whiles Metropolis Waste Management Department pay the remaining 50% (¢30) charge (KMA – WMD, 2017) to reduce the cost burden on clients and to curb solid waste management menace in the metropolis. Therefore, on the monthly basis, the total cost incurred on both waste collection and disposal by the private waste management companies in the metropolis amounts to ¢2,160,000 (1200 tonnes × 30 days × ¢60) assuming 1200tonnes of solid waste is collected per day. This total cost comprises of fuel cost, vehicle spare parts and servicing, salaries, allowances and profits of the private waste management companies. The KMA-WMD on the other hand is financed by the Metropolitan assembly and other NGOs whiles Private waste management companies are financed with income generated from clients or service utilisers. KMA-WMD is however mandated to provide logistics (waste bins, sanitary boots, gloves, nose cap etc) to the Private Waste Management Companies for effective and efficient service delivery in the metropolis.

Sometimes clients are also provided with waste bins like skips and containers at a cost by the KMA-WMD. Also waste containers are sometimes provided at demarcated sanitary sites in CBDs for waste collection. However, the waste containers at the CBDs are not protected from the weather and are emptied once a week but used to be twice a week. This issue is attributed to inadequate logistics and calls for the provision of more vehicles and equipment by the Assembly and waste management companies to undertake the collection process. Operationally, source separation and recycling of solid waste is encouraged by the Metropolis Waste Management Department (MWMD) however the department is not willing to give incentives to clients for source separation.

Organic waste constitute 40-50% of the total solid waste collected in the metropolis (KMA-WMD, 2017) but the assembly does not have recycling units which do not facilitate recycling. Also the assembly has no sanitary stations except the demarcated areas for private waste management companies. Recently, people are contracted to sort out solid waste in the metropolis and it is very effective however, the department has no recovery and processing strategies in solid waste management. Therefore all unsorted solid waste ends up at the landfill site which is 10 kilometres away from the Metropolis Waste Management Department's (MWMD) office. This landfill site is owned by the metropolis but currently managed by a private waste management company, Kumasi Waste Management Limited. Also Trucks loaded with solid waste for disposal are mostly covered but do not undergo any treatment at the landfill site.

Even though 80% of waste management has been outsourced to the private sectors according to government policy, other options could have been considered if any but due to inadequate equipment there is no other option available now. Outsourcing is very good to the metropolis but has two side effects in terms of sustainability. Firstly, the strategy is sustainable and very helpful because the companies help out a lot in terms of solid waste management therefore relieving some financial and social burden from the Kumasi Metropolitan Assembly Waste Management Department. However, it may not be sustainable because the private waste companies are profit oriented and may not help in their operation in the long run which will lead to high cost burden on the clients as time goes on. Their services are also rated average in the metropolis especially in the CBDs and there is more room for improvement. Furthermore, due to absence of waste bins at advantageous points especially in the CBDs, ineffective sanitation bye laws and human attitude, the streets of the metropolis are always littered making solid waste management in busy areas tedious.

According to Head of Research and Development at KMA WMD during an interview, she stated that, "*Even though KMA WMD has financial challenges, bins are also not necessary because people will still litter anyway*". The Assembly therefore stated that "*We have plans to push all cost burdens on solid waste management to the general populace*" (KMA-WMD, 2017). The assembly also has bye laws governing waste management. Even though, education is done on the sanitation regulations, bye-laws and the adverse effects of keeping dirty environment, it is done seasonally; especially during the rainy seasons because of inadequate funds. Sanitary inspections are also done once in a while the Environmental Health and Sanitation Unit officers in the metropolis.

4.3 EXAMINING INSTITUTIONAL FRAMEWORK GOVERNING SOLID WASTE MANAGEMENT AND HOW ITS CONFORMITY IS AFFECTED BY FINANCE

The stakeholders of solid waste management in the metropolis include government, EPA, EHSD, MMDA's, private waste management companies and the clients. The government is in charge of policy formulation and award of contracts; EPA is the environmental safety regulators, EHSD enforces environmental bye-laws and the

MMDA's is in charge of monitoring and supervision of solid waste management activities. The set-up of regulations and byelaws for solid waste management work very well except that its enforcement is on the decline. Some of the bye laws for clients include; no burning of refuse and no indiscriminate dumping. Negative attitude and negligence are factors that grossly affect sanitation issues in the country. However people engage in indiscriminate dumping due to inadequate education, unavailability of receptacles for waste and avoiding payment for waste collection. Attitude and negligence make it difficult to manage solid waste properly. Most often people engage in indiscriminate dumping of solid waste when it becomes difficult to pay for the waste they generate and poor understanding of waste disposal. This can adversely lead to disasters example flood and outbreak of diseases. However, these attitudes can be curbed by regular education, enforcement of environmental sanitation byelaws and prosecuting culprits by the Assembly.

Other duties of the stakeholders include the public generates the waste; the contractors collects the waste and the KMA regulates the services and provides landfill site for disposal even though the landfill site is managed by the Kumasi Waste management Company Limited. Some of the institutional guidelines or bye laws enforced by the KMA include the need to have standard working equipment to work with; and the need to maintain all central containers by the contractors. However, according to the operations' manager of Asadu royal seed and waste management Ltd, inadequate funds make it impossible to acquire and maintain this equipment to deliver services according to set standards. Also operation's manager of Kumasi Waste Management Ltd complained about inadequate knowledge on how the institutional guidelines or bye laws governing the companies are enforced. According to the operations manager at Kumasi Waste Management limited,

"I am not sure of how the regulatory and byelaws work in the company and I have not seen any institutional guideline or bye laws enforced by the KMA in solid waste management".

The KMA incurs no cost to adhere to waste management standards. Even though the regulatory framework is cumbersome and mandatory, the waste management companies do not abide by them at a go, and it takes time to meet all the standards and requirements. Some of the regulatory are environmentally motivated and capital intensive because it involves huge investment to meet the standard. However since there is not much pressure to meet all the standards at the start of operations, solid waste management companies are good to commence operations and work their way throughout the consecutive years.

Also clients at the public utility services like market centers and bus terminals do not incur cost in abiding by the sanitation bye-laws because they are not being regulated or sanctioned for the bad attitude towards sanitation and hygiene in these places. The feedback from the respondents indicates that 97% of the markets facilities and bus terminals have never being sanctioned for keeping a dirty or unclean environment. This shows the reason why the users keep on littering around and do not keep a clean and healthy environment. However, the situation is not the same at the household and residential areas because waste generators are sanctioned for keeping unclean environments.

Table 4.9 Facility sanction for Keeping Unclean Environment

Response	Frequency	Percentage (%)
Yes	2	3
No	58	97
Total	60	100

Source: Field Survey, 2017

4.4 EXPLORING THE POTENTIAL FINANCIAL RESOURCES AT THE DISPOSAL OF WASTE MANAGEMENT INSTITUTIONS

Occasionally, KMA receives financial support from foreign organisations like the French Development Agency (AFD) but these sources of funds are not always reliable because they are received as and when there are sanitation programmes and projects on board internationally and there is a need for positive change in sanitation issues. Generally, the source of funds for solid waste management in the metropolis is from the clients or users of public facility and it is mobilised through the payment of facility user fees (tolls). During the study, it was realised that public facility users' tolls have been increased because sanitation charges have been factored into it.

Currently, the private waste companies pay ¢30 per tonne of solid waste disposed-off at the landfill site to the KMA whiles the tricycle operators pay ¢15 per tricycle of solid waste disposed-off at the landfill site. Clients are also charged an average of ¢30 a month for house to house collection and the charge depends on the amount of solid waste generated by each household. Whiles clients who utilise communal containers at sanitary sites pay between ¢1 - ¢3 depending on the quantity of waste disposed-off. However, at the market places and bus terminals there is a fixed amount charged from facility users; facility users at the market pay ¢0.50 individually per day whiles vehicles drivers pay between ¢1-¢5 individually on weekly basis.

Some of the potential source of funds for the waste department may include increasing public facility users' daily toll (ticket) charges since sanitation charges are being factored into it, increasing tipping fees by private waste companies at the landfill site and increment in tricycle operators' charges for disposal. Increment in these charges are however affected by the quality of services delivered to clients and the willingness of the clients to pay the current amount been charged.

Also private waste management companies can recycle organic solid waste into organic manure or compost and sell to the agricultural sector and farmers as organic fertilizers to serve as another source of income for solid waste management. Plastics can also be recycled into waste bins and sold out for cash to support management cost. Other disposed-off items like car tyres, metallic barrel, ceramic and artefacts can be recycled into useful furniture for household and commercial use as well as decorations at aesthetic environments. Solid waste can also be converted to energy (biogas) for sale and other purposes. Investments into other profitable ventures in the environmental conservation sector can also be another source of funds for both KMA and private waste management companies. Finally, increment in service charges to clients.

These sources of funds may be important to the operations of solid waste management companies and the waste management department of the metropolis however challenges like unwillingness of clients, tricycle operators, private waste management companies and clients to pay increased charges can hinder the potential source of fund to the Assembly. Also the unwillingness of foreign investors and Non-Governmental Organisation to support the Assembly can be a major problem. Again the capital intensiveness of recycling can also prevent private waste management companies from engaging in recycling even though it may be profitable in the long run.

Some possible ways to counteract these challenges include; upgrading the informal status of tricycle operators with the KMA to a semi-formal status which requires them to meet certain standards in operation, give the tricycle operators a sense of belongingness into the solid waste management stream and acknowledge their efforts/importance towards keeping clean and health environments in the metropolis. On the part of private waste management companies, the assembly have to fulfil their part in provision of the necessary logistics to them to make their work effective and efficient. When this provision is made, it cuts the cost burden on the companies in acquiring these logistics and the available funds can be used for logistics maintenance for efficient delivery services and investment into other profitable ventures in the environment and sanitation sector. Finally, the sanitation services provided by the assembly through private waste management companies at the public facilities must be thoroughly monitored by the assembly to ensure efficient service delivery and a clean environment in these areas. An interview with one of the managers of the bus terminal at central market (Dr Mensah) revealed that "*the clean-up of the station has being halted since 2008 and they have to pay for the services of a contracted cleaner at a cost of ¢30 per day even though the facility pays tolls to the assembly every day. Each vehicle pays ¢3 to the assembly excluding revenue tax and facility user fees*"

Attracting foreign investors into the waste management stream of the assembly will be fruitful only when the assembly put the mobilised funds from clients in to efficient service delivery systems and waste management processes. When the assembly fulfils their part of the quota to the private waste management companies and clients, the impact will be felt in the solid waste management system which will give a positive feedback to world for more investments and waste management projects like large scale recycling in the metropolis.

67

4.5 ASCERTAINING THE CHALLENGES TO CURRENT STATE OF FINANCING IN SOLID WASTE MANAGEMENT

Private waste management companies do not receive financial support from other organisations therefore their operations are financed through service charges paid by clients, loans from financial institutions and other investments by the companies. These sources of funds are however challenged in different dimensions such as high operation cost and unwillingness of clients to pay for services delivered.

4.5.1 Financial Analysis of Solid Waste Management Companies

Based on data collected from waste management companies, financial analysis was made for companies who willingly gave out their financial strength information. These companies include SAK-M and Asadu Royal Seed and Waste Management Company Limited.

SAK-M Waste Management Company

Due to inadequate information on the flow of income to this company, the revenue for only two years was recorded as at the time of study. In 2015, the company received total revenue of ¢480,000 and ¢408,000 for the year 2016 and there was no specific figures allocating to the collection systems even though the source of funds is from the clients. This therefore did not give a clear definition of the sources of revenue. The trend of expenditure is indicated in Table 4.10

Table 4.10 Expenditure trend for SAK-M Waste Management Company

Components of Expenditure Amount in cedis (¢)	2012	2013	2014	2015	2016	Total
Fuel	158,760	166,698	175,032	183,783	192,972	877,245
Administrative	269,640	283,122	297,278	312,142	327,749	1,489,931
Operations	124,800	129,792	134,984	140,383	147,402	677,361
Total	553,200	579,612	607,297	636,308	667,123	3,043,540

Source: Field Survey, 2017

From the expenditure table 4.10 administrative charges constitute a larger percentage (48.7% - 49.1%) of the expenses followed by fuel expenditure (28.7% - 28.9%) and lastly operations (22. 1% - 22.6%). The profitability analysis in Figure 4.1 indicated a loss to the company as the expenditure line is seen above the revenue. This shows that the company has been operating on loan or deficit financing from the year 2015-2016 which is detrimental to the sustainability of its delivery of service at the catchment area. Currently, most of the public facilities in their catchment area have been left unattended to for solid waste collection due to inadequate staff and breakdown of waste collection trucks. The few remaining trucks are used by the company to collect solid waste from the manufacturing companies in the area because they serve as the main source of funds for operation. This fund is also being used to repair broken down trucks and maintain the remaining staff and has rendered the company ineffective in delivering service to the public facilities users for some time now. There is a pertaining issue of delayed solid waste collection in the area due to inadequate logistics and human resources. The company has also proposed to lay off some of its workers to reduce the administrative cost even though the workers are not enough to undertake the current daily waste collection in the catchment area which will adversely affect its operations more. The profitability analysis of the company was done using two years (2015 and 2016) because data on revenue for the period 2012 to 2014 was not available based on the company's records.

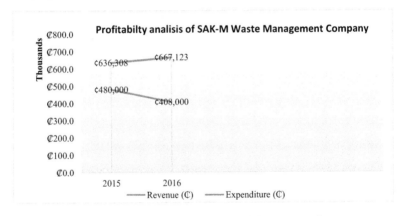

Figure 4.1 Profitability Analysis of SAK-M Waste Management Company

Source: Field survey (2017)

The revenue and expenditure flow of the company is represented in Table 4.11 and Table 4.12 respectively for analysis. From the revenue Table 4.11, the major sources of fund for the company are from the clients and the house to house collection system contributes much to the revenue stream as compared to the communal collection system. This is because, in the house to house collection, clients waste are collected as they pay however the communal system, even though the people who utilise are many, the overriding factor is disturbing since some client dump their waste at odd hours where they are not seen to be charged for disposal.

Table 4.11 Revenue inflow of Asadu Royal Seed and Waste Management Company Limited

Sources of finance / Amount in Cedis (₵)	2013	2014	2015	2016	2017	Total
Houses to house collection	578,760	627,060	654,020	660,300	699,250	3,219,390
Communal collection	266,760	304,440	330,240	343,440	357,120	1,602,000
Total	845,520	931,500	984,260	990,740	1,056,370	4,821,390

Source: Field Survey, 2017

From the expenditure table 4.12, fuel expenses constitute the highest expenditure in the company's operation, followed by vehicle parts and maintenance expenditure and lastly administrative expenditure. The profitability analysis however showed a high profit accrual since the revenue of the company outweighs the expenditure. This indicates a high sustainability of efficient service delivery in the company's catchment area. The company however is majorly engaged in house to house collection therefore its service impact is felt mostly in the households but not the communal services. However the few public facilities that utilises their services can boast of good sanitation and environmental condition. An example is Ayigya market.

Table 4.12 Expenditure Trend of Asadu Royal Seed and Waste Management Company Limited

Components of Expenditure / Amount (Cedis)	2013	2014	2015	2016	2017	Total
Parts and Maintenance Expenditure	157,260	169,890	188,100	201,540	214,980	931,770
Administrative Expenditure	112,720	134,023	148,005	171,216	201,740	767,704
Fuel Expenses	164,027.04	192,163.16	232,054.08	280,052.64	328,045.44	1,196,342.36
Total	434,007.04	496,076.16	568,159.08	652,808.64	744,765.44	2,895,816.36

Source: Field Survey, 2017

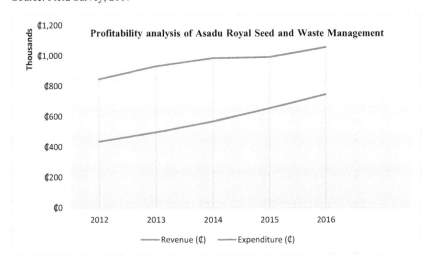

Figure 4.2 Profitability Analysis of Asadu Royal Seed and Waste Management Company Limited

Source: Field survey, (2017).

4.5.2 Challenges

Currently, solid waste management companies are challenged financially due to unwillingness of clients to pay charges and high cost of operations. Adequate financial resources auger well for waste management within the metropolis and vice versa however high dumping charges deter people from dumping at sanitary sites and even securing a bin which resort to indiscriminate dumping.

71

Insufficient funds make it difficult for some of the companies to replace old vehicles to enable them operate effectively and compete with other waste management companies. These companies are also faced with the challenge of non-payment of fees and unavailability of direct funds from banks due to bad shape of collateral security and high risk of debit financing. Some of the companies also have improper system of recording revenue and expenditure for financial statement. According to operations manager at SAK-M, *"Our operations are funded with money charged from clients. Other sources of funds include; bank loans and government payments. Due to inadequate funds, we can't buy trucks and access loans sometimes due to low inflow of funds"*.

The challenges encountered in operations at the catchment areas include; non-payment of monthly fees, frequent breakdown of vehicles due to leach and acidic content in the waste. Poor road network, inadequate bins, low and delay payment of charged fees, high cost of waste trucks and other equipment, and poor implementation of contract agreement by KMA. The solid waste management companies also complained of poor road networks and streets linkages as a hindrance to effective delivery of services. According to Asadu Royal Seed and waste management company Limited *"We are faced with numerous challenges in operation within our catchment areas and these include; poor accessibility (Streets/roads) to houses, unwillingness of clients to pay charges and register with the company"*

The major problems militating against waste collection in the catchment areas include high operational cost and ineffective revenue mobilisation. Other challenges also include pressure to work, trucks, financial constraints and technical knowhow. As indicated in the table 4.13 the major challenge faced by the facility users is the absence of waste bins.

Table 4.13 Challenges users face in managing wastes

Challenges	Frequency	Percentage (%)
Inadequate better containers	52	87
Others	8	13
Total	60	100

Source: Field survey, 2017

Customers Satisfaction for Service Delivery

Access to current sources of fund is also affected by satisfaction derived from sanitary services provided by companies. According to respondents, the facilities are cleaned mostly by users, organised labour and Zoomlion. Even though they know the assembly is supposed to take charge of the clean-up, they see it appropriate for users to also take part. Despite the challenges facility users encounter in keeping clean environment, the facilities are appropriately cleaned before the beginning of the days' activities. This is done in a manner that after the nights' sweep up by the contracted cleaners especially in the markets; the facility users do a second sweep up in the morning to start the day's work. However some users insisted on the assembly taking charge as they feel it is not their responsibilities to do so and they also pay for the services.

Table 4.14 People Responsible for Facility Clean-up

Organisation	Frequency	Percentage (%)
Zoomlion	14	23
Organised Labour	16	27
Individual users	9	15
Others (Specify)	21	35
Total	60	100

Source: Field Survey, 2017

Clean up of facilities is done daily and especially in the mornings for less busy facilities and in the evenings for very busy facilities. Facility users also pay for waste collection and disposal. The waste is collected daily to avoid unpleasant scenes however; there is still a huge gap in doing that. Waste collection is however mostly done by tricycle operators and other contracted labour at a fee even though payments made to the assembly is supposed to cover these charges. The markets centres also resort to "Kayaye" for waste collection when it is not done by the KMA or Zoomlion. Since the daily clean up by the facility users is burdensome and waste collection is not effective in the current situation, some of the facility users expressed their profound interest to contract any other informal contractors that will deliver a better service at an affordable rate.

Table 4.15 Response on payment for solid waste collection by facility users

Response	Frequency	Percentage (%)
Yes	53	88
No	6	10
No response	1	2
Total	60	100

Source: Field Survey, 2017

Table 4.16 Waste collection organisations

Organisation	Frequency	Percentage (%)
District assembly	2	3
Private wagons	20	33
Zoomlion	11	18
Others (Specify)	24	40
Not applicable	3	5
Total	60	100

Source: Field Survey, 2017

It was realised that bus terminals and taxi ranks in commercial areas had a big challenge in waste disposal and collection. Because these facilities do not pay directly to the private waste management companies, the delivery of services is not satisfactory and the facility users and managers are compelled to bare another cost for contracting or organising back up labour to keep the facilities clean. But this is not the case in the less busy and private owned bus terminals since these facilities had a controlled level of activities and proper system of waste disposal and collection. These facilities are however taken care of by paid organised labour or specially contracted waste management companies.

Plate 4.14 Adum Harper Road Taxi Station
Source: Field Survey, 2017

Plate 4.15 Bus Terminal at Central
Market (Dr. Mensah)

Plate 4.16 Bus Terminal at Old
Kejetia.

Source: Field survey, 2017

Plate 4.17 STC Bus Terminal, Adum

Plate 4.18 VIP Bus Terminal, Asafo

Source: Field survey, 2017

All the cleaning charges of the residential and commercial markets on the other hand are taken care of by the assembly except in some case where users have to pay for solid waste collection as a back-up service or obligation. Whiles private owned markets have paid contractors who clean and collect solid waste at a cost charged from store owners and paid by market managers.

Plate 4.19 Central market, Urvan (Trotro) station, (Borla)
Source: Field survey, 2017

Willingness to pay

Solid waste management companies charge a price for solid waste collection and wish to increase the price but the clients are not willing to pay additional charges except where private waste management companies deliver services according to expectations of clients. However tricycle operators are highly challenged in this situation since they are not formally recognised by clients therefore subjecting them to unfavourable terms and compliance with clients. They pay for waste disposal at the landfill site and the distance to the landfill site affects the cost of their operation and charges.

Table 4.17 Receptiveness of clients to pay collection fees

Receptiveness to payment	Frequency	Percentage
Willing to Pay	1	10
Not willing to pay	8	80
Indifferent	1	10
Total	10	100

Source: Field Survey, 2017

Table 4.18 Willingness of Companies to Increase Collection Fee

Response	Frequency	Percentage
Yes	6	60
No	4	40
Total	10	100

Source: Field Survey, 2017

76

4.6 ANALYSING HOW EXISTING FINANCING MECHANISMS AND RESOURCES CAN BE SUSTAINABLY USED TO MANAGE SOLID WASTE

The current sources of finance for solid waste management available to institutions have been the major funds for all solid waste management processes in the metropolis and have contributed significantly to the sanitation situation however it is still not enough because the issue of poor sanitation still exist in the metropolis. These inadequacy of funds put sanitation institutions at tight corners while they thrive to meet sanitation standards and better solid waste management processes and service delivery systems. To ensure effective and efficient use of these funds and avoid embezzlement of fund, there should be proper systems put in place in organisations by the managers for better accounting, accountability and improved financial statement to help waste management companies keep track records of their financial gains and loss for the appropriate measures to be put in place to ensure good financial strength. A good financial record of the companies will give them credibility and good image in the sight of financial institutions which will grant them easy access to loans in the future.

Secondly, there should be profitable use of bank loans to develop business and pay back on the agreed terms and conditions. Funds taken from financial institutions are mostly used to pay workers' salaries whiles companies' logistics are inadequate or in bad shape. Companies should therefore set their priorities right in the development of their organisations in terms of operations, logistics stock and administrative cost to know which will give them much profit when invested in to offset operations and administrative cost whiles paying for acquired loans within the time frame.

There should also be effective use of revenue from clients to improve upon the quality of service delivered to them. When quality services are delivered clients will be willing to pay more for the good work done. Again profit accrued in the bumper seasons should be invested in profitable ventures to yield the companies more sources of funds for operations. These profits can be invested in the solid waste management process like giving clients incentives for waste separation to facilitate and promote recycling.

4.7 CONCLUSION

Financing is a major challenge in every organisational structure and may affect operations negatively or positively notwithstanding the management system. The solid waste management structure in the metropolis is no different in this section.

Due to inadequate funding, the solid waste management processes have been disrupted and inconsistent in delivery of services by waste management companies and the metropolis waste management department. This has led to the unclean and unhealthy environment witnessed by many in the urban CBDs, market places and bus terminals. This situation needs appropriate measures put in place to curb the resulting effects of inadequate financing on sanitation and environmental issues in the metropolis.

CHAPTER FIVE

FINDINGS, CONCLUSION AND RECOMMENDATIONS

5.1 INTRODUCTION

This part of the study highlights the major findings with their implications, conclusion and recommendations drawn from the findings. It recommends cutting-edge strategies to financing solid waste management in the metropolis as population increases.

5.2 SUMMARY OF FINDINGS

This section talks about findings discovered on the general and specific objectives of the study. In relation to the solid waste management the sources of solid waste identified by the study were classified as municipal as it dealt with solid waste management in commercial areas like markets and bus terminals. It also revealed the financial challenges and prospects of solid waste management in the metropolis for effective and efficient delivery of services to the people to solve the sanitation menace in the CBDs.

5.2.1 Ascertaining Financial Contribution of Stakeholders in Solid Waste Management in the Metropolis

Practically, KMA waste management Department has no financial obligation towards private waste management companies except to provide them with logistics for smooth operation. The KMA has also planned to shift all cost burden of solid waste management in the metropolis to service utilisers/customers in the near future. However, this is under gradual process even though the clients serve as the major source of funding to the solid waste management companies currently. This strategy of cost bearing will help the customers to be more conservative in consumption and reduce the rate of waste generation whiles adopting Integrated solid waste management. It was also realised that the efficiency in solid waste management delivery services depends on the location of the facilities, the level of activities undertaken in the facilities and the willingness to pay for charges of contracted services providers.

The KMA-WMD is however financed by the Assembly through the mobilised revenue from public facility users and some NGOs (occasionally) for special sanitation and environmental projects like KEEP KUMASI CLEAN AND GREEN initiated in 2018 whiles private waste management companies operators are financed by client charges, loan acquired from banks and other profitable investments by the companies. Tricycle operators are also financed by clients' charges. The KMA however do not provide private waste management companies with the needed logistics for effective operations in the designated public facilities in their operation zones.

5.2.2 Examining How Conformity to Institutional Framework Governing Solid Waste Management is affected by Finance

Adherence to solid waste management standards and regulatory is highly affected by finance. Both clients and solid waste management companies find it difficult to go by the regulatory and bye laws due to financial issues. Whilst companies give preference to clients who pay for services, clients who cannot afford payment for services resort to negligence and indiscriminate dumping.

Even though adherence to set standards would have accrued more profit for the solid waste management companies through better delivery of services to clients according to EPA and KMA standards, inadequate funds is not making that possible. Some of the institutional guidelines or byelaws enforced by the KMA include the need to have standard working equipment to work with, and the need to maintain all central containers by contractors. Inadequate funds make it impossible to acquire and maintain this equipment to deliver services according to set standards. Also the tricycle operators operate in the informal sector with little regulations so they presume it is not obligatory to adhere to certain standards

It was also realised that, because CBDs, market places and bus terminals are not sanctioned for keeping unclean environments they do not see the need to keep clean environment. Also the work of private waste management in these areas is not efficient because they are not frequently monitored and supervised on their contracted works at the sub metros.

5.2.3 Potential Sources of Funds for Waste Management Institutions

Some of the potential sources of funds identified for the waste management department include increased clients' charges, increased tipping fees at the landfill site and increment in tricycle operators' charges for disposal. Whiles the potential sources of funds for private solid waste management companies include sales of recycled solid waste example, organic manure or compost from organic waste products, recycled plastics into waste bins and furniture, and conversion of waste to energy for sale amongst others.

However since the clients are not satisfied with the services delivered to them at the facilities, they are reluctant to pay the current charges which makes it difficult to increase it. Also the tricycle operators operate in the informal sector and they are less informed about the operation systems and contract agreements between the KMA-WMD and private waste management companies. Therefore increment in their charges seems a threat to them and as strategy by the KMA to push them out of business.

Also there are conflicting issues with operations within the sub metros between tricycle operators and private waste management companies as tricycle operators trespass companies' zones for customers. The KMA-WMD not providing companies with the necessary logistic coupled with the conflict with tricycle operators hinder increment in disposal charges at the landfill site.

Again, the Assembly and companies are not fully engaged in the recycling and environmental projects because of its capital intensive nature but they wish to venture into this field in the near future if they get more funds to support operations. Even though, they are seeking for funds the KMA and the companies have not engaged in any significant environmental and sanitation projects for a very long time now to attract investors.

5.2.4 Challenges to Current State of Financing in Solid Waste Management

Currently, the solid waste management companies are challenged financially due to unwillingness of clients to pay charges and high cost of operations. Adequate financial resources promotes waste management within the metropolis and vice versa however high dumping charges deter people from dumping at sanitary sites and even securing a bin which resort to indiscriminate dumping. The average total monthly cost of transportation and disposal of solid waste by companies is between ¢30,000 and ¢40,000. The average monthly operations cost for the contracted companies amounts to ¢89,000 which include expenses on fuel, spare parts, vehicle servicing, salaries, PPE's etc. and they charge between ¢15 to ¢40 for house to house collection and as low as ¢1 for communal collection based on the quantity of the waste collected for disposal from customers. The tricycle operators on the other hand spend an average of ¢1,867.50 on monthly operations.

This expenditure coupled with unwillingness of clients to pay for service delivery is detrimental to the sanitation situation of the metropolis. Trespass by tricycle operators in the operation zones of companies is also detrimental to their sources of funds. This is because tricycle operators have flexible system of operation and the clients feel comfortable to bargain with them which always favour the client at the end.

Most of the companies rely on bank loans to finance their operations. However, the absence or bad shape of collateral securities makes it difficult to access these loans especially when the companies have been running on overdraft for a long period of time. This has an adverse effect on the delivery of services by companies in their catchment areas.

It was realised that most of the companies do not keep track record of their operating expenses and revenue so it was difficult to make financial analysis for them. This improper system of financial record does not help business development and gives the companies bad status to acquire loans from banks.

5.2.5 Analysing How Existing Financing Mechanisms and Resources Can Be Sustainably Used To Manage Solid Waste

The study revealed that most of the waste management companies including the KMA-WMD are not involved in significant environmental conservation and sanitation projects to support their work and to boost their financial strength. Waste management companies like Asadu Royal Seed and Waste Management Company LTD and Zoomlion Ghana LTD are involved in seed nursing farm projects and small scale recycling (in Greater Accra) respectively. The KMA and other private companies are however engaged in collection and disposal of solid waste only which is not encouraging.

It was realised that bank loans acquired by private waste management companies are mostly used to offset administrative cost instead of operation cost which does not help the companies in the short and long run. Loans from banks can be used to acquire new logistics and maintain the old ones for efficient sanitation services to clients which will help improve upon the customer satisfaction derived from the services delivered.

Despite the amount paid by clients, it was realised that, the services delivered were not satisfactory in the CBDs therefore do not encourage the facility users to pay for the service delivered because they are bare additional cost of contracting back up services to collect solid waste gathered in their facilities for disposal.

5.3 CONCLUSION

The companies who maximise profit in the long run are those whose major operations are house to house and communal collection but the companies involved in the public services at the CBDs and other busy commercial areas stand the risk of incurring loss in the long run due to insufficient fund which result to poor sanitation issues. Inadequate funds is the cause of poor sanitation issues in busy commercial areas because the rate of waste generation in these areas is very high which demand frequent collection and disposal but is not possible due to inadequate logistics.

Provision of both small and bigger waste bins at advantage points with convenient intervals in CBDs, market places and bus terminal is cost intensive since waste bins and containers are provided at zero cost to the clients. The cost burden on companies become heavy to bear which in turn hinders them from delivering quality services. These issues coupled with clients' unwillingness to pay for the current price and proposed increment is determined by the quality of service provided by companies. Companies should endeavour to deliver efficient services for a better fee chargein the midst of the financial challenges.

5.4 RECOMMENDATION

Waste generation in the metropolis is proportional to population growth which implies that waste will always be generated. Therefore to reduce waste generation, the 3Rs (Reduce, Re-use and Recycling) should be key and effective. Even though, solid waste treatment has been started by Zoomlion Ghana Limited there is more room for improvement and other companies are encouraged to engage in these processes because it is another source of revenue stream. Although it might be capital intensive from the beginning, the cost may be recovered and profit maximised in the long run. Some recovery and processing strategies used by the company include; plastic recovery and processing into litre bins and bin liners.

5.4.1 Ascertaining Financial Contribution of Stakeholders in Solid Waste Management in the Metropolis

The Kumasi Waste management department and private waste management companies must be ready to give incentives to clients to promote source separation and recycling of solid waste as it has been encouraged by the metropolis and gradually being accepted by the people. Thus a client must have more than one bin to separate waste into organics, plastics, papers, etc to improve the value chain of waste. Incinerating to generate energy and composting of organic waste must also be encouraged since organic waste constitute majority of waste.

Generally, the system of engaging external collectors is sustainable only when adequate resources are available for collection. Notwithstanding, waste collected should be put to good use and not disposed-off at landfills. There should be conversion of waste to energy treatment plant provided by the Assembly that collects all organic waste to recover energy which can be sold to augment logistical resources needed to manage solid waste effectively.

The assembly should be committed in payment of mobilised public service user fees to support the private waste companies in charge of clean up, waste collection and disposal in the commercial areas to employ more people to undertake clean up exercises and acquire more logistics for waste collection and disposal.

Clients must be educated by the Assembly on the importance of payment for service delivery by waste management companies and tricycle operators since it is the major source of fund for their operation and other sources of funds available to these companies through the metropolitan assembly should be made available to them to promote efficient delivery of service. Whiles accessing funds, the companies must also deliver quality services which will entice clients to pay the charged fees and be ready to accept any future increment in fee paying. Solid waste collection system can be improved by letting the public regularly pay the right amount or charge thus the full cost for their waste at the end of the month to the contractors if the local government is not willing to pay the subsidy.

5.4.2 Examining How Conformity to Institutional Framework Governing Solid Waste Management is affected by Finance

The initiative started by the metropolis through KEEP KUMASI CLEAN AND GREEN project which provides waste bins at advantage points in metropolis must be sustained. The assembly should also fulfil their part in the provision of the required logistics to waste management companies to promote efficiency in service delivery.

Again the people should be educated on how to handle waste and all contract regulations in contracting private waste management companies signed with the KMA must be followed. To solve these problems, the public must be educated and sensitised by the assembly and should provide logistics such as skip bins and central waste containers at the sanitary sites.

The work of private waste management companies in the public facilities must also be supervised and monitored by the KMA to ensure efficient solid waste management service delivery in the metropolis. Facility users can also be sanctioned for keeping dirty environments to keep them on their toes to have clean environments good for commerce.

Formalisation of tricycle operators will help improve upon their operating system and keep them accountable for some solid waste management malpractices they undertake. Especially off-loading their collected solid waste at areas with already gathered solid waste for collection by private waste management companies in the public facilities. This will help to avoid free riding and misunderstanding between clients and solid waste management companies

5.4.3 Potential Sources of Funds for Waste Management Institutions

The KMA-WMD and Private Waste Management Companies must be ready to invest in other profitable sectors in relation to environmental conservation through waste management to boost their financial strength. They must work on the appropriate strategies to sort out and recycle solid waste collected into useful end products. To help mobilise, access and manage funds for solid waste management, generated waste should be given value to pay for its management resources. They must also come out with innovative sanitation and environmental ideas and projects frequently to attract investors for business support, proper solid waste management and healthy environment.

Solid waste management companies in collaboration with the KMA-WMD must endeavour to deliver satisfactory services to their clients to motivate them pay for the current charges and proposed future increment. Formalisation of tricycle operations by the KMA will help to improve their operations for more revenue. When tricycle operators are well informed about the contract terms of solid waste management by the KMA, their involvement in solid waste engagement will be boosted. As a resultant effect, they will apply efficient strategies to support the bigger companies in their work instead of operating as competitors.

5.4.4 Challenges to Current State of Financing in Solid Waste Management

Banks should not only give loans based on the collateral securities of the companies but based on their ability to pay back loans on the agreed terms and conditions depending on the number of years the bank has transacted with the companies. This will help to build trust among the companies and financial institutions to help them in times of financial difficulties. Companies should also keep proper accounting system for a good financial record which will help them to acquire loans from banks and give them investor confidence as well.

Private waste management companies must also get a flexible system of payment for their clients to bridge the gap filled by tricycle operators. This will also help them to increase their customer base for larger revenue.

5.4.5 Analysing How Existing Financing Mechanisms and Resources Can Be
Sustainably Used To Manage Solid Waste

The loans acquired from banks by waste management companies can be used for significant investments (recycling, acquisition of new vehicles and vehicle maintenance) which will help develop the business to pay back granted loans on the agreed terms and conditions within the loan repayment time

Finally, there must be a clearly defined policy framework on effective waste management that encourage waste to value technologies. There should also be tax rebates on importation of logistics for waste management.

REFERENCES

Addaney, M., & Oppong, R., A. (2015). Critical Issues of Municipal Solid Waste Management in Ghana. JENRM 2(1): 30-36.

Addo, E., A. (2009). Economic Analysis of Household Source Separation of Solid Waste: The Case of Kumasi Metropolis of The Ashanti region of Ghana. MPhil Thesis in Agricultural Economics, KNUST

Adomako-Adjei, T. (2008). Scaling Up Sanitation Delivery: The Perspective of Community Water and Sanitation Agency. Ghana: WEDC

Adu-Boahen, A., K. (1975). Ghana: Evolution and change in the 19th and 20th Centuries. London, Longman.

Adu-Gyamfi, E., (2014). Effective Revenue Mobilisation by Districts Assemblies: A Case Study of Upper Denkyira East Municipal Assembly of Ghana. Public Policy and Administration Review 2(1):97. Published by American Research Institute for Policy Development

Agbola, T. (1993). Environmental Education in Nigerian Schools. In: Filho, W.L., Ed., Environmental Education in the Commonwealth, the Commonwealth of Learning, Vancouver.

Ahorlu, W., K. (2006). Managing Waste in Africa – A Look at Institutional Constraints, Hazardous Waste and Public-Private Partnership Options.

Akrani, G. (2011). What Is Finance? Meaning Definition Features of Finance. http://kalyan-city.blogspot.com/2011/11/what-is-finance-meaningdefinition.html

Amoaning, R. (2006). Sanitation - Our Collective Responsibility. Presentation at CONIWAS-DANIDA. Workshop; Kumasi, Ghana.

Anomanyo, E., D. (2004). Integration of Municipal Solid Waste Management in Accra University of Ghana (Ghana) Bioreactor Treatment Technology as An Integral Part of The Management Process. Presented to Lund University, Sweden.

Aoki, M. (2001). Toward A Comparative Institutional Analysis. Cambridge: MIT Press, 2001

Armah, N., A. (1993). Waste Management: The Future of Our Cities. Proceedings of The Ghana Academy of Arts and Sciences, 28(78-83).

Asase, M., A., D. (2011). Solid Waste Separation at Source: A Case Study of The Kumasi Metropolitan Area. A Thesis Submitted To The Chemical Engineering Department, Kwame Nkrumah University Of Science And Technology, Kumasi, In Partial Fulfilment Of The Requirements For The Degree Of Doctor Of Philosophy, Faculty Of Chemical And Materials Engineering, College Of Engineering

Attahi, K. (1999). Metropolitan Governance in Abidjan. Seminar on Development and Urban Africa. Centre d'Estudis Africans, Barcelona.

Blaike, P. & Brookfield, H. (1987). Land Degradation and Society. London: Methuen. Xxiv +269 Pp. £10.95 Paper.

Blaikie, P., & Brookfield, H. (1987). Land degradation and society. New York: Methuen.

Boadi, K., O., & Kuitunen, M. (2004). Municipal Solid Waste Management in The Accra Metropolitan Area. The Environmentalist 23(3): 211-2118

Boateng, C., & Nkrumah, D. (2006). Managing Waste! The Attitudinal Change. Daily Graphic, 16th December, P (20).

Buba, A. (2013). Recycling Biodegradable Waste Using Composting Technique. 4(40 – 49).

BusinessDictionary.com (2017). Management. Retrieved December 18, 2017, from Business Dictionary.com website: http://www.businessdictionary.com/ definition/ management.html

Centre for Environment and Development (2003). Study of The Attitude and Perception of Community Towards Solid Waste Management: A Case Study Of Thiruvananthapuram city-Phase II. Kerala Research Programme on Local Level Development.

Chandra, Y., I., & Linthoingambi N. (2009). Studies on Municipal Solid Waste Management in Myosore City: A case study. http://www.sciencepub.net.

Coffie, O., Drechsel, P., Obuobie, E., Danso, G., & Keraita, B. (2003). Environmental Sanitation and Urban Agriculture in Ghana: Towards the Millennium Development Goals. Nigeria, Abuja, WEDC, 2003, 9-12.

Cointreau-Levine, S. (1994). Private Sector Participation in Municipal Solid Waste Management Services in Developing Countries – (1). The Formal Sector, UNDP/UNCHS/The World Bank – Urban Management Programme.

Cointreau-Levine, S. (2001). Declaration of Principles for Sustainable and Integrated Solid Waste Management.

Damoah, A. (2011). Improving Refuse Collection in District Assemblies Through Outsourcing to Private Agents: A Case Study of Kumasi Metropolitan Assembly.

Danso, K., B., M. (2011). The Nature of Solid Waste Management in Ghana: Towards Data Collection for Good Management Practices. http://www.google.com/ webhp?hl=en#hl=en&q=The+Nature+of+Solid+Waste+Management+.

Dapaah, A. S. (1989). Sustainability of Technical Assistantance Projects. Journal of Management Studies, Vol 5

Denison, R., A., & Ruston, J. (1990). Recycling and Incineration. Island Press, Washington D.C.

Denzin, N., K. (1989). The Research Act: A Theoretical Introduction to Sociological Methods (3rd Edition). New Jersey, Prentice Hall

Department of Environment and Land Management (DELM), (2003). Tasmanian Hazardous Waste Strategy.

Devas, N., & Korboe, D. (2000). City Governance and Poverty: The Case of Kumasi. Environment and Urbanization. (12)1:123-136.

Downmore, M., Shepherd M., Andrew M., Barbara N. & Daniel J. (2011). Municipality Solid Waste (MSW) Management Challenges Of Chinhoyi Town In Zimbabwe: Opportunities Of Waste Reduction And Recycling.

Drucker, P. F. (November 19, 1909 – November 11, 2005). What is management? http://www.whatishumanresource.com/what-is-management

EGSSAA (2009). Environmental Guidelines for Small-Scale Activities in Africa http://www.encapafrica.org/EGSSAA/solidwaste.pdf.

El-Fadel, Mutasem et al. (1997). Environmental Impacts of Solid Waste Landfilling. Journal of Environmental Management. 50(1): 1-25. Emission Standards Division.

Environment Council, UK (2000). The waste guide: The stakeholders guide to sustainable waste management. London, Environment Council.

Environmental Health and Sanitation Directorate (2010). National Environmental Sanitation Strategy and Action Plan NESSAP: Materials in Transition MINT. 23(142). Ministry of Local Government and Rural Development, Ghana.

Mohammed, F. (2008). The Dilemma of Sanitation Coverage in Ghana. Water, Sanitation, Environment and Development, Ghana: WEDC, 1: 50-53.

GEPA (2002). Ghana Landfill Guidelines. Environmental Protection Agency of Ghana. Ministry of Environment Science and Ministry of Local Government And Rural Development.

Ghana Environmental Protection Agency (2002). Newsletter. (5):2 July-December 2002. Accra. EPA.

Ghana Innovation Marketplace (2009). Waste Management Conference and Exhibition. 11th-12th November, 2009. Great Hall, KNUST.

Ghana Statistical Service (2011). Ghana Population and Housing Census. Ghana Statistical Service, Accra.

Ghana Statistical Service (2012). 2010 Housing and Population Census Report. Accra, GSS.

Ghana Statistical Service (2012). Final Report on Population and Housing Census, Accra. Sakoa Press Limited.

Ghana Statistical Service (2012). Population & Housing Census Summary Report Of Final Results.

Ghana Statistical Service (2014). Population and Housing Census, District Analytical Report. Kumasi Metropolitan Assembly.

Gourlay, K., A. (1992). World of Waste (Dilemmas of Industrial Development). 2nd edition. Books Ltd., 57 Caledonian Road, London, 21-49.

Hoornweg, D., & Bhada-Tata, P. (2012). What A Waste: A Global Review of Solid Waste Management. Urban Development Series Knowledge Paper No. 15

Hueting R. (1980). New Scarcity and Economic Growth: More Welfare through Less Production? Amsterdam: North Holland Publishing Company. Original Dutch edition published by Agon Elsevier, Amsterdam, 1974.

Karki, S. (2010). Risk Sharing Key Benefit of Outsourcing Utility Services, Continuity Central Journal. http://www.continuitycentral.com/news0760.htm

Kendie, S. (1998). Employment Structure and The Environment in Cape Coast, Ghana. Singapore Journal of Tropical Geography. 19. 26 - 38. 10.1111/ j.1467-9493.1998. tb00248. x.

Kendie, S., B. (1998). Do Attitudes Matter? Waste Disposal and Wetland Pollution in The Cape Coast Municipality of Ghana. Malaysian Journal of Tropical Geography, 29(2), 69-81 University of Bradford, England.

Ketibuah, E., Asase M., Yusif S., Mensah, M.Y. & Fischer, K. (2004). Comparative Analysis of Household Waste in the Cities of Stuttgart and Kumasi - Option for Waste Recycling and Treatment in Kumasi. Proceedings of the 19th international CODATA Conference, 1-8.

Knowledge Management Terms. (2009, January 20).Retrieved from Stuhlman Management Consultants: http://home.earthlink.net/~ddstuhlman/defin1.htm

Kreith, F. (1994). Handbook of solid waste management. McGraw Hill, USA.

Kumah, A., M. (2007). The situation of solid waste in Ghana. Accra, Ghana.

Kumasi Metropolitan Assembly (2006). District Medium Term Development Plan, Kumasi Metropolitan Authority.

Kumasi Metropolitan Assembly (2012). Domestic Waste Management Strategies and Implementation in Kumasi 2009 – 2012.

Kumasi Metropolitan Assembly Waste Management Department (KMA) (2010): Data For Purposes Of Planning Waste Management Intervention Programmes, Kumasi Waste Management Department. Kumasi, Ghana

Kumekpor, K., B., (2002). Research Methods & Techniques of Social Research, Ghana. Son Life Printing Press and Services.

Kurt, D., (2019). What is Finanace? Investopedia. https://www.investopedia.com/ask/answers/what-is-finance/

Kwarteng, S., O., & Van Dijk, M., P. (2008). Performance of Private Companies Involved In Urban Solid Waste Management: Evidence From Three Cities In Ghana. IN:Jones,H.(ed) Access To Sanitation And Safe Water: Global Partnership And Local Actions: Proceedings of the 33rd WEDC International Conference Accra., Ghana 2008 pp.114-120.

Lohse, U. (2003). Improving Municipal Finance – A Global Challenge. Habitat Debate, Innovative Urban Financing. UN-HABITAT 9(1).

Martin, O., A. (2011). Governance Crisis Or Attitudinal Challenges? Generation, Collection, Storage And Transportation Of Solid Waste In Ghana. Integrated Waste Management. Intech 1 (978- 953-307-469-6).

Menegat, R. (2002). Paticipatory Democracy and Sustainable Development: Integrated Urban Environmental Management in Porto Alegre, Brazil. Environmental and Urbanisation 14 (2): 181-206

Mensah, A., & Larbi E. (2005). Fact Sheet Solid Waste Disposal (SWD) in Ghana. www.trend.watsan.net.

Miller, D. (1999). `Social Justice. New York. Oxford University Press.

Ministry of Environment and Forestry Notification (MEFN) (2000), New Delhi.

Ministry of Local Government and Rural Development (MLGRD) (2004). National Environmental Sanitation Policy: The Expanded Sanitary Inspection and Compliance Enforcement (ESICOME) Programme.

Ministry of Local Government and Rural Development (MLGRD) (2010). Strategic Environmental Sanitation Investment Plan (SESIP). Accra, Ghana: Government of Ghana.

Ministry of Local Government and Rural Development (1999). Environmental Sanitation Policy. Government of Ghana.

MOFA-KMA. (2009). http://mofa.gov.gh/site/?page_id=859

Momoh, J., J., & Oladebeye, D., H. (2010). Assessment Of Awareness Of Attitude And Willingness Of People To Participate In Household Solid Waste Recycling Programme In Ado-Eketi, Nigeria. Journal Of Applied Sciences In Environmental Sanitation; Jakarta, Indonesia.

Monney, I., Makimula T., B. & Chendire B., H. (2013). Characteristics And Management Of Household Solid Waste In Urban Areas In Ghana: The Case Of WA. Civil And Environmental Research. 3. 10-21.

Nandomah, S., Abuku W. D., & Bogpae, J. Y., (2015). Assessing The Efficiency Of Segregating Solid Waste At The College Of Science, KNUST. A Dissertation Submitted To The Department Of Environmental Science, Kwame Nkrumah University Of Science And Technology In Partial Fulfilment Of The Requirement Of The Degree Of Bachelor Of Science In Environmental Science.

Oduro-Kwarteng, S., Awuah E., & Kotoka P. (2006). Solid Waste Management Practices In Kumasi, Ghana: Public Concerns And Attitudes Towards Disposal And Cost Recovery. http://www.google.com.gh/search?q= Odurokwarteng%2 C+S.%2C+Awuah+E%2C+and+Kotoka+P.%2C+%282006%29.&ie=utf8&oe =utf8&aq=t&rls=org.mozilla:enUS:official&client=firefoxa.Accessed;10h May, 2012

Ofori, R. A. (2013). Integrated Waste Management-Source Separation And Composting Of Household Waste In The Ayuom Farming Community In The Bosomtwe District Of The Ashanti Region

Ogawa, H. (2002). Sustainable Solid Waste Management In Developing Countries. WHO Western Pacific Regional Environmental Health Centre (EHC). Kuala Lumpur,Malasia. Accessed at: http://www.gdrc.org/eem/waste/swm-fogawa1. htm. 13/02/11

91

Ogawa, H. (2005). Sustainable Solid Waste Management in Developing Countries (www.gdrc.org.).

Onibokun, A., G., & Kumuyi, A., J. (1999). Ibadan, Nigeria. Onibokun, A.G. (Ed). Managing the Monster. Urban Waste and Governance in Africa, 1- 12.

Pacione, M. (2005). Urban Geography. A Global Perspective 2nd Edition. London and New York, Routedge, Taylor & Francis Group.

Palczynski, R., J., & Scotia, W., N. (2002). Study On Solid Waste Management Options For Africa. Project Report, Prepared For African Development Bank Sustainable Development and Poverty Reduction Unit, Abidjan. Final Draft Version.

Post, J., & Obirih-Opareh, N. (2003). Partnerships And The Public Interest: Assessing The Performance Of Public-Private Collaboration In Solid Waste Collection In Accra. Space And Polity, 7(1): 45-63.

Post, J., Broekema, J. & Obirih-Opareh, N. (2003). Trial And Error In Privatisation: Experience In Urban Solid Waste Collection In Accra (Ghana) And Hyderabad (India). Problems And Building Successes. GTZ Urban Studies 40 (4):835-852

Scheinberg, A., Wilson, D., & Rodic-Wiersma, L. (2010). Solid Waste Management in the World's Cities, UN-HABITAT.

Schubeler, P., Wehrle, k. & Christen, J. (1996). A conceptual Framework for Municipal Solid Waste Management in Low-Income Countries, UMP Working Paper Series 9, UMP/SDC SKAT, Geneva, 15-51.

Schubeller, P. (1996). Urban Management And Infrastructure: Conceptual Framework For Municipal Solid Waste Management In Low-Income Countries. Collaborative Programme On Municipal Solid Waste Management In Low-Income Countries. St, Gallen, SKAT. Working Paper 9. UNDP/UNCHS /Habitat/ World Bank/SDC

Tagoe, N., Nyarko, E., & Anuwa-Amarh (2005). Financial Challenges Facing Urban Smes Under Financial Sector Liberalisation In Ghana. Journal Of Small Business Management, 43(3): 331-343.

Tchobanoglous G. (2003). Solid Waste Management. Civil And Environmental Engineering. University Of California. ISBN 0-471-41813-7 _ 2003 John Wiley & Sons, Inc., Hoboken, New Jersey.

Tchobanoglous, G., Theisen, H. & Eliason, R. (1977). Solid Wastes: Engineering Principles And Management Issues. McGraw-Hill Publishing Company, USA.

Tchobanoglous, G., Theisen, H. & Vigil, S. (1993). Integrated Solid Waste: Engineering principles and management issues. McGraw-Hill Publishing Company, USA.

Tsiboe, A. & Marbell Q. (2004). An Analysis of Solid Waste Management in Accra, Ghana. Master's Thesis, Roskilde University, 13-14.

U.S. EPA. EPA's Report On The Environment (ROE) (2008 Final Report). U.S. Environmental Protection Agency, Washington, D.C., EPA/600/R-07/045F (NTIS PB2008-112484), 2008.

United Nations Environmental Programme (2000). Global Water Supply and Sanitation Assessment 2000 Report.

United Nations Environmental Programme (2004-5). Environmental Management And Community Participation - Enhancing Local Programmes. Nairobi, Kenya.

United Nations Environmental Programme (2005). Selection, Design And Implementation Of Economic Instruments In The Solid Waste Management Sector In Kenya: The Case Of Plastic Bags. UNEPETB, Geneva.

United Nations Environment Programme (2005). ISBN: 92-807-2643-9 Job No.: DEW/0746/NA

United Nations Environmental Programme (UNEP) (2009). Assessment of Current Waste Management Systems and Gaps Therein: Developing Integrated Solid Waste Management Plan Training Manual (2). United Nations Environmental Programme Division of Technology, Industry and Economics International Environmental Technology Centre Osaka/Shiga, Japan.

United States Environmental Protection Agency (1999). National source reduction characterization report for municipal solid waste in the United States. EPA 530R-99-034, Office of Solid Waste and Emergency Response, Washington, D.C

United States Environmental Protection Agency (USEPA)(1999). State and Local Solutions to Solid Waste Management Problems.USEPA, New York, USA

Urban Sector Programme Support Secretariat (2000). Solid Waste Management Plan for Thimphu City, Bhutan. Bhutan, Urban Sector Programme Support Secretariat, Drafted Version.

Vodounhessi, A. (2006). Financial And Institutional Challenges To Make Faecal Sludge Management Integrated Part Of ECOSAN Approach In West Africa: Case Study Of Kumasi, Ghana. Msc Thesis WM 2006.05, UNESCO-IHE Institute For Water Education, Delft, The Netherlands.

Web Governments (2011). Solid Waste Management. Ghana. http://webgovernments .wordpress.com/2011/12/08/solid-waste-management-ghana.

WELL Fact Sheet (2005). Solid Waste Disposal in Ghana. file:/// C|/ Web page /LRA/LOGISTIC REGRESSION ANALYSIS.htm (1 of 9)

World Bank (1999). What a Waste: Solid Waste Management in Asia Urban Development Sector. International Bank for Reconstruction and Development N.W. Washington, D.C., U.S.A

World Bank (2002). World Bank urban solid waste management: Private sector involvement. http://www.worldbank.org/urban/uswm/private sector.html.

World Bank (2012). What A Waste: A Global Review On Solid Waste Management; Urban Development Series; Washington D.C. www.dec.ny.gov/ chemical/ 8486.

World Bank, (2001). What a Waste! Solid Waste Management in Asia. Accessed at http:// www.bvsde.paho.org/bvsacd/cd48/wasteasia.pdf.

Zerbock, O. (2003). Urban Solid Waste Management: Waste Reduction in Developing Nations. www.cee.mtu.edu.

Zoomlion Ghana Limited (2010). Field Survey on Solid Waste in Kumasi Metropolitan Assembly, Ashanti Region.

Zurbrugg, C. (2002). Solid Waste Management In Developing Countries. SANDEC/ EAWAG.

Zurbrugg, C. (2009). Solid Waste Management In Developing Countries. www. sanicon.net.

APPENDICES
APPENDIX I
RESEARCH QUESTIONNAIRE FOR HEADS OF MARKET USERS ASSOCIATIONS AT MARKET CENTERS

This research is designed to see relevant data for academic purpose (awarding of Masters' degree) for the year 2017. Your support and cooperation would be very much appreciated. Please tick where appropriate and state where necessary (applicable).

(N.B. Any information given would be held highly confidential)

SECTION A DEMOGRAPHIC CHARACTERISTICS

Questionnaire Number...

Market Section ....

1. Respondent's name ....

2. Gender

    1. Male [ ] 2. Female [ ]

3. Level of respondent's education

    1. Illiterate [ ]

    2. Primary [ ]

    3. Junior high [ ]

    4. Senior high [ ]

    5. Tertiary [ ]

SECTION B WASTE MANAGEMENT

4. Who is responsible for cleaning the surroundings of this section of the market?

    1. The district assembly [ ]

    2. Zoomlion [ ]

    3. Organised labour [ ]

    4. Individual users [ ]

    5. Others (Please specify)............................

5. Is the clean-up appropriately done?

    1. Yes [ ] 2. No [ ]

6. If no, what should be done to ensure appropriate clean up?

....

....

7. Is it appropriate for facility users to clean the surroundings?

    1. Yes [ ] 2. No [ ] 8. If no why?

    1. Inadequate time [ ]

95

2. Not our responsibility [ ]

3. Not our responsibility but.........................

9. How often are the surroundings cleaned?

    1. Daily [ ]

    2. Weekly [ ]

    3. Every two weeks [ ]

    4. Once a month [ ]

10. What do the users of this facility use to collect waste before disposal?

    1. Basket [ ]

    2. Wooden box [ ]

    3. Polythene bag [ ]

    4. Bucket [ ]

    5. Pan [ ]

    6. Dustbin [ ]

    7. Zoomlion containers [ ]

    8. Others (Specify).......

11. Do you sort waste before disposal?

    1. Yes [ ]

    2. No [ ]

12 If yes why do you sort? ....

13. If no why?

    1. Inadequate time [ ]

    2. Unhygienic [ ]

    3. Difficult [ ]

    4. Insignificant [ ]

    5. Other .....

14. Can solid waste be recycled? 1. Yes [ ] 2. No [ ]

15. Where do market users dispose-off waste?

    1. Open space [ ]

    2. Zoomlion wagons [ ]

    3. Pit [ ]

    4. Dustbins [ ]

    5. Others ....

16. When do market users normally dispose-off wastes?

    1. Morning [ ]

2. Afternoon [ ]

3. Evening [ ]

4. Anytime [ ]

17. Are there waste containers placed at vantage points at the market centre? 1. Yes [ ]

2. No [ ]

18. Is the refuse container big enough for waste collection?

1. Yes [ ] 2. No [ ]

19. Do the waste containers overflow?

1. Yes [ ] 2. No [ ]

20. If yes how often?

1. Most often [ ] 2. Sometimes [ ] 3. Rarely [
] 21. 21. Do you pay as you dump refuse?

1. Yes [ ] 2. No [ ]

22. If yes, how much? Gh¢......... per............

23. What challenges do the facility users encounter in managing waste?

1. Time barrier [ ]

2. Distance barrier [ ]

3. Inadequate funds [ ]

4. Inadequate proper bins [ ]

5. Other [ ]

24. Does the facility users pay for solid wastes to be collected from the facility? 1. Yes [ ] 2. No [ ]

25. **If yes,** who collects the wastes?

1. District Assembly [ ]

2. Private wagons [ ]

3. Zoomlion [ ]

4. Others (Specify)..........................

26. How much do you pay? Gh¢ ....daily/weekly/monthly

27. How often is the waste collected?

1. Everyday [ ]

2. Every week [ ]

3. Fortnights [ ]

4. Monthly [ ]

28. If no (25), would you like your solid waste to be collected from your facility?

1. Yes [ ] 2. No [ ] 30. If no, why?

1. Facility can dispose it off [ ]

2. For re-use [ ]

3. Facility cannot afford collection cost [ ]

4. Waste collectors are not reliable [ ]

5. Others (Specify) ....

29. If yes, who will the facility employ to collect waste?

1. Zoomlion [ ]

2. Facility users [ ]

3. District Assembly [ ]

4. Others (Specify) ....

30. Any reason for the choice made?

....

....

31. How much will facility pay for waste collection by a contracted service provider?

Gh¢.........per...........

32. What other duties does the waste collectors perform aside collecting and dumping off waste?

....

....

33. Is the facility summoned or sanctioned for keeping dirty environment?

(1). Yes   (2). No

34. If **yes**, what was the punishment?

35. Other comments ....

APPENDIX II

RESEARCH QUESTIONNAIRE FOR MANAGERS AT BUS TERMINALS

This research instrument is designed to seek relevant data for academic purpose (awarding of Masters' degree) for the year 2017. Your support and cooperation will be very much appreciated. Please tick where appropriate and state where necessary (applicable).

(N.B. Any information given would be held highly confidential)

SECTION A DEMOGRAPHIC CHARACTERISTICS

Questionnaire Number..

Name and location of bus terminal ....

Respondent's name ....

1. Gender

    1. Male [ ] 2. Female [ ]

2. Level of Education

    1. Illiterate [ ]

    2. Primary [ ]

    3. Junior high [ ]

    4. Senior high [ ]

    5. Tertiary [ ]

SECTION B WASTE MANAGEMENT

3. Who is responsible for cleaning the surroundings of the bus terminal?

    1. The district assembly [ ]

    2. Zoomlion [ ]

    3. Organised labour [ ]

    4. Individual users [ ]

    5. Others (Please specify)..............................

4. Is the clean-up appropriately done?

    1. Yes [ ] 2. No [ ]

5. If no, what should be done to ensure appropriate clean up? ....

6. Is it appropriate for facility users to clean the surroundings?

    1. Yes [ ] 2. No [ ]

7. If no why?

    1. Inadequate time [ ] 2. Not our responsibility [ ]

    3. Not our responsibility but ....

8. How often is the surrounding cleaned?

1. Daily [ ]

2. Weekly [ ]

3. Every two weeks [ ]

4. Once a month [ ]

9. What does the terminal use to collect waste before disposal?

1. Basket [ ]

2. Wooden box [ ]

3. Polythene bag [ ]

4. Bucket [ ]

5. Pan [ ]

6. Plastic dustbin [ ]

7. Zoomlion containers [ ]

8. Other (Specify)....... [ ]

10. Do you pay from solid waste to be collected from facility? 1. Yes [ ] 2. No [ ]

11. If yes, who collects waste?

1. District Assembly [ ]

2. Private wagons [ ]

3. Zoomlion [ ]

4. Others (Specify)...........................

12. How much do you pay Gh¢............ per day/week/month? How much do you pay?

13. How often is waste collected?

1. Daily [ ]

2. Weekly [ ]

3. Every two weeks [ ]

4. Every month [ ]

14. If no, would you like solid waste to be collected from facility?

1. Yes [ ] 2. No [ ]

15. If no, why?

1. Facility can dispose it off [ ]

2. For re-use [ ]

3. Facility cannot afford collection cost [ ]

4. Waste collectors are not reliable [ ]

5. Others (Specify) ....

16. If yes, who will you employ to collect waste?

1. Zoomlion [ ]

2. Facility users [ ]

3. District Assembly [ ]

4. Others (Specify) ....

17. State one reason for your choice

....

....

....

18. How much will you pay for waste collection? Gh¢ ....per ....

19. Do you sort waste before disposal?

1. Yes [ ]   2. No [ ]

20. If yes, why do you sort? ....

21. If no, why?

1. Inadequate time [ ]

2. Unhealthy [ ]

3. Tedious [ ]

4. Not important [ ]

5. Others .....

22. Do you know some of the waste can be recycled?

1. Yes [ ]   2. No [ ]

23. Where do you dispose-off waste?

1. Open public dump [ ]

2. Zoomlion wagons [ ]

3. Pit [ ]

4. Dustbins [ ]

5. Others ....

24. When do you normally dispose-off waste?

1. Morning [ ] 2. Afternoon [ ] 3. Evening [ ] 4. Anytime [ ]

25. Do you think waste containers are placed at advantage points? 1. Yes [ ]   2. No [ ]

26. Do the waste containers overflow?

1. Yes [ ]   2. No [ ]

27. If yes how often?

1. Most often [ ]   2. Sometimes [ ]   3. Rarely [ ]

28. Is the container too high up?

1. Yes [ ]   2. No [ ]

29. Do you pay to dispose-off refuse?

1. Yes [ ]   2. No [ ]

30. If yes, how much? Gh¢...........per ....

31. Is the refuse dump/container very far from the facility?

1. Yes [ ]   2. No [ ]

32. What challenges do you face in managing waste?

1. Time factor [ ]

2. Distance barrier [ ]

3. Finance [ ]

4. Inadequate proper containers [ ]

5. Other [ ], specify ....

33. Has the terminal being sanctioned before for keeping a bad environment

1. Yes [ ]   2. No [ ]

34. If yes what was the punishment? ....

35. Who instigated the punishment? ....

RESEARCH QUESTIONNAIRE FOR PRIVATE WASTE MANAGEMENT COMPANIES

This research Instrument is designed to seek relevant data for academic purpose (awarding of Masters' degree) for the year 2017. Your support and cooperation would be very much appreciated. Please tick where appropriate and state where necessary (applicable).

(N.B. Any information given would be held highly confidential)

SECTION A

Questionnaire Number...

1. Company ....

2 .Position of the respondent ....

3. Do you think it is prudent for the KMA to outsource refuse collection?

    1. Yes [ ]   2.No [ ]

4. If yes why?

....

....

5. If no why?

....

....

6. How long has your company been involved in waste management in the assembly?

    1. Below 1year [ ]

    2. Between 1 to 4 years [ ]

    3. Between 5 to 9 years [ ]

    4. Between 10 to 14 years [ ]

    5. Above 15 years [ ]

7. Has the company been contracted by KMA been contracted by KMA to support waste management in the assembly?

    1. Yes [ ] 2. No [ ]

8. If yes, for how long has your company been contracted to support good sanitation maintenance in the Kumasi metropolis by the KMA.

    1. Below 5years [ ]

    2. Below 10 years [ ]

    3. Below 15 years [ ]

    4. Above 15 years [ ]

9. Has your company been able to meet your mandate of refuse collection as agreed in the contract you signed with the KMA?

    1. Yes [ ] 2. No [ ]

10. Do you think the assembly's engagement with your firm has been beneficial to the Kumasi metropolis?

    1. Yes [ ] 2. No [ ]

11. Has the assembly been prompt in their payments to your organization for the services they have contracted you to provide?

    1. Yes [ ] 2. No [ ]

12. In your opinion how sustainable is this strategy of engaging external vendors like you to aid refuse collection projects in the metropolis?

....

....

13. Which other strategy will you suggest to be considered by the assembly in waste collection aside outsourcing to private companies?

....

....

14. What other waste management functions do you perform aside solid waste collection?

....

....

SECTION B

15. Coverage area (Name of Sub-metro Covered) and size

....

....

16. What time of the day do you collect the waste?

    1.   Morning [ ] 2. Afternoon [ ] 3. Evening [ ] 4. Other (specify)

....

17. What is the method of waste collection from clients?

    1.   House to house collection [ ]

    2.   Communal collection [ ]

    3.   Other, specify.....................................

18. How many houses make a vehicle full in waste collection?

    1.   50-100 [ ] 2. 100-150 [ ] 3. 150-200 [ ] 4. Above 250 houses [ ]

19. How many houses contribute to waste collection containers at sanitary site?

    1.   50-100 [ ] 2. 100-150 [ ] 3. 150-200 [ ] 4. Above 250 houses [ ]

20. How many vehicles do you use in waste collection at coverage area?

....

21. Are there other forms of transport used for the collection of waste?

    1.   Yes [ ] 2. No [ ]

22. If yes, specify

....

....

23. Does the company provide waste bins to clients?   1. Yes [ ] 2. No [ ]

24. If yes, which ones? ....

25. How many waste bins per client?

    1.   1 [ ]   2. 2 [ ]   3. 3 [ ] 4. More than 4

26. How much does a waste bin cost?   ....

27. If no why? ....

28. Do you have any suggestions to improve upon collection system?

    1.   Yes [ ] 2. No [ ]

29. If yes specify

....

....

30. How often do you collect waste from house to house or sanitary site?

    1.   Daily [ ]   2. Weekly [ ]   3. Others, specify ....

31. How many times can a vehicle collect waste to landfill in a day?

    1.   One [ ]   2. Two [ ]   3. Three [ ]   4. Other

....

32. Does the company charge collection fee? 1. Yes [ ] 2. No [ ]

33. If yes, how much do you charge?

1. House to house collection rate? ....

2. Communal collection rate? ....

3. Market rate? ....

4. Bus terminal rate? ....

34. What standard does the company use in charging fee? ....

35. How receptive is the payment of fees by clients?

    1. Willing to pay [ ]   2. Not willing to pay [ ]   3. Indifferent [ ]

36. Do you wish to increase the cost of collection fees?

    1. Yes 2. No

37. How much does the company spend in waste collection every month?

Gh¢...........................

38. What account for cost?

39. What is the major problem militating waste collection in coverage area?

....

....

40. Which recommendations will the company give to promote effective waste collection?

....

....

41. Do you encourage source separation at waste collection? 1. Yes 2.No [ ]

42. If yes what type of waste dominate?

....

....

43. Would the company be willing to give incentives for source separation by clients?

    1. Yes [ ] 2. No [ ]

44. If yes, what is the monthly estimates for these incentives?

....

....

45. Does the company cover waste trucks with net? 1. Yes [ ]   2. No [ ]

46. If no, why and when do you intend to do so? ....

47. How many sanitary sites are within the coverage area?

....

....

48. How are the sanitary sites designated?

....

....

49. Who does the designation of the sanitary sites?

1. KMA [ ]   2. EPA [ ]   3. Private Waste Companies [ ] 4. Others (Specify)

....

51. How many collection containers are placed in each sanitary site?

1. One [ ]   2. Two [ ] 3. Three [ ] 4. Above three ....

52. What activities are undertaken at sanitary sites?

53. Are central waste containers protected from the weather? 1. Yes   2. No [ ]

54. How often are these containers emptied?

1. Rarely   2. Daily   3. Every two days   4. Weekly   5. Monthly

55. Where is waste taken to from the sanitary sites?

1. Recycling center [ ]

2. Compost recovery [ ]

3. Incineration [ ]

4. Landfill [ ]

56. What is the estimated cost of solid waste transfer by the company (daily/weekly/monthly)?

....

....

57. Does the company have a recycling unit?

1. Yes [ ] 2. No [ ]

58. If yes how the recycling done?

....

....

59. If no why and where does your recycling take place?

....

....

107

60. If yes, what is the estimated cost of recycling by the company, daily/ weekly /monthly?

....

61. Are there ways to reuse waste? 1. Yes [ ]   2. No [ ]

62. If yes how?

....

63. If no why?

....
....

64. Does the company own a Landfill?

      1. Yes [ ] 2. No [ ]

65. If yes (in 64), where is the landfill? ....

66. If No, where do you dump your waste?

....
....

67. How far is collection point to disposal point? ....km

68. Does the distance to landfills determine cost of transportation and disposal?

1.   Yes [ ]   2. No [ ]

69. If yes how much does transportation and disposal of waste cost the company in a month? Gh¢..

70. Do you pay fees before disposing off waste at landfill? 1. Yes 2. No [ ]

71. If yes, how much? ....

72. If no, why? ....

73. Do you receive any financial support from other organisations?

      1. Yes [ ]   2. No [ ]

74. If Yes which organisations do you receive support from?

....
....

75. If no how do you finance solid waste management?

....
....

76. What support must the government give to sustain private sector participation in solid waste management?

....
....

SECTION C – INSTITUTION, FINANCE AND LOGISTICS
INSTITUTIONAL FRAMEWORK

1. Who are the stakeholders in this company?

....

....

2. What are the roles of various stakeholders in this company?

....

....

3. What institutional framework govern provision of services in solid waste management?

....

....

4. How does the set up regulatory and byelaws work for solid waste management in this company?

....

....

5. What are some of the institutional guidelines or byelaws enforced in the KMA concerning waste management in this company?

....

....

6. How does attitude and negligence affect sanitation issues?

....

....

7. Why do people engage in indiscriminate dumping of waste?

....

....

8. What do you think can be done about it?

....

....

FINANCE

9. What are the available financial resources at the disposal of your company?

....

....

10. How does the company access financial resources for its operation?

....

....

11. How does finance affect adherence to solid waste management standards and regulatory

....

....

12. How does finance affect sanitation issues in the metropolis?

....

....

13. How can the available sources of fund be mobilised, accessed and managed to finance solid waste management to ensure healthy living environment in the metropolis?

....

14. What are the effects and challenges of the company in the current state of financing waste management?

....

15. What is the amount and flow of funds for operations from the year 2012 to 2016?

Sources of finance / Amount in Cedis	2012	2013	2014	2015	2016

16. What is the pattern of expenditure from the year 2012 to 2016?

Components of Expenditure / Amount (Cedis)	2012	2013	2014	2015	2016

WASTE MANAGEMENT

1. What is the current process for solid waste management used by the company?

   ....

   ....

2. What are the recovery and processing strategies in waste management used by the company?

   ....

   ....

3. What are the sources of solid waste in the metropolis?

   ....

   ....

4. What percentage is the waste composition in the metropolis?

   ....

   ....

5. How can the waste generation be reduced in the metropolis?

   ....

   ....

6. Which people are engaged in sorting of solid waste for the company?

   ....

   ....

7. How receptive is sorting in the metropolis and what are the processes used by the company?

   ....

   ....

8. What percentage of solid waste is recycled by the company?

   ....

   ....

9. What percentage of solid waste is sent to landfill by the company?

   ....

   ....

10. How are the current pertaining challenges on waste management curbed?

   ....

   ....

RESEARCH QUESTIONNAIRE FOR WASTE MANAGEMENT STAFF AT THE KUMASI METROPOLITAN ASSEMBLY

This research instrument is designed to seek relevant data for academic purpose (awarding of Masters' degree) for the year 2017. Your support will be very much appreciated. Please tick where appropriate and state where necessary (applicable). *(N.B. Any information given would be held highly confidential)*

SECTION A

Questionnaire Number...

Date of Interview (DD/MM/YY)........../............./2017

1. Gender of interviewee

    1. Male [ ] 2. Female [ ]

2. Department of the assembly

....

....

3. Rank in the Department

....

....

4. Years of service

    1. 1 – 4 [ ]   2. 5 – 9 [ ]   3.10 – 14 [ ]   4. 15 – 19 [ ]   5. 20 – 29 [ ]   6. 30 + [ ]

5. What do you think is/are the cause(s) of poor sanitation in Kumasi?

    1. Attitudinal [ ]   2. Cultural [ ]   3. Poor education [ ]   4. Governmental [ ]   5. Financial [ ]

6. Other (Please state)...........................

7. Who is responsible with keeping the city clean?

    1.   Local Government [ ]   2. Individuals [ ]   3. Both [ ]   4. Other (Please state)....................

8. What is the present approach used by the KMA waste management department in managing waste in the Kumasi metropolis? ....

9. Do you think the approach to waste management is good enough?

    1. Yes [ ]   2. No [ ]   3. Maybe [ ]

10. Do you believe outsourcing to private waste management companies is the best option in dealing with waste management in the Kumasi metropolis?

    1. Yes [ ]   2.No [ ]   3.Maybe [ ]

11. If yes why? ....

12. If no why?

....

....

13. What other options can the KMA consider in dealing with waste management in the city apart from outsourcing? Specify ....

14. Is Outsourcing to private waste management companies as a strategy for improving refuse collection in the metropolis sustainable?

   1. Yes 2. No

15. If yes how?

....

....

16. If no why?

....

....

17. Why do you think the assembly opt for outsourcing waste collection to a private investor?

   1.   Financial [ ] 2. Inefficiency [ ] 3. Good will [ ] 4. Politics [ ] 5. None of the above [ ]

18. How will you rate service provided by private waste management Companies in the Metropolis?

   1. Very bad 2. Bad 3. Average 4. Good 5. Very good

Reason for the answer

....

....

19. Has there been improvement in the sanitation of the metropolis prior to outsourcing in their areas apportioned?

   1. Yes [ ] 2. No [ ]

Reason for the answer...

20. Why do you think littering the streets of the metropolis is common?

   1.   Absence of dustbins

   2.   Human attitude

   3.   Ineffective sanitation bye laws

21. Reasons for the answer chosen in question 19?

   1.   Lack of goodwill of the KMA to provide bins [ ]

   2.   Financial constraints [ ]

   3.   Bins are not necessary because people will still litter anyway [ ]

4. Others ....

22. What do you suggest to be done to solve the issue of littering around?

    1.   The KMA should provide bins to collect waste in town at whatever cost to stop littering [ ]

    2.   The KMA should hire agents to clean/collect litter or refuse in town [ ]

23. How do you think waste management can be better improved in the city?

....

....

24. Whom do you think should pay for sanitation maintenance in the metropolis?

    1. Government [ ] 2. Individuals [ ] 3. Both [ ] 4. Others (Specify)

....

....

25. Does the assembly have bye-laws on solid waste management?

    1. Yes [ ] 2. No [ ]

26. If yes, do the people in the metropolis know about them?   1. Yes [ ] 2. No [ ]

27. Do you organise educational programmes on proper waste management in the metropolis? 1. Yes [ ] 2. No [ ]

28. If yes, how often does educational take place?

    1. Daily [ ] 2. Weekly [ ] 3. Monthly [ ] 4. Others......

29. If no, why?

1. Financial constraints [ ] 2. Inadequate staff [ ] 3. Lack of political will [ ] 4. Others ....

30. How frequent are Sanitary Inspection on waste management undertaken in households at the metropolis?

    5. Daily [ ] 2. Weekly [ ] 3. Monthly [ ] 4. Once in a while

31. What are the reasons for irregular inspections?

    6. Financial constraints [ ] 2. Inadequate staff [ ] 3. Political instability [ ]   4. Other reasons [ ]

32. What is the major challenge faced by the Metropolis in managing solid waste?

    1. Financial constraints 2. Inadequate staff 3.Inadequate containers

    4. Indiscriminate dumping of refuse 5. No sorting 6. Others ....

SECTION B – INSTITUTIONAL, FINANCIAL AND LOGISTICS

INSTITUTIONAL FRAMEWORK

1. Who are the stakeholders involved in waste management in the metropolis?

....

....

2. What are the roles of various stakeholders/institutions in solid waste management in the metropolis?

....

....

3. What are the institutional framework governing solid waste management in the metropolis?

....

....

4. How does the set up conditions for solid waste in the metropolis work?

....

....

5. What are the institutional guidelines or byelaws enforced in the KMA concerning waste management?

....

....

6. How are these bye laws enforced in metropolis and by who?

....

....

7. How does attitude and negligence affect sanitation issues?

....

....

8. Why do people engage in indiscriminate dumping of waste?

....

....

9. What do you think can be done about it?

....

....

FINANCE

10. What are the available financial resources at disposal of the waste management department?

....

....

11. How does the department access financial resources for its operations?

....

....

12. How does finance affect sanitation issues in the metropolis?

....

....

13. Are there any potential sources of funds for waste management in the metropolis?

1. Yes [ ] 2. No [ ]

If yes, list them

....

....

14. How can potential sources of fund be mobilised, accessed and managed to finance solid waste management to ensure healthy living environment in the metropolis?

....

....

15. What are the effects and challenges of the current state of financing waste management?

....

....

16. How much does it cost KMA to adhere to solid waste management standards

....

....

WASTE MANAGEMENT

17. What amount of waste was generated from 2010-2017 in KMA daily, weekly, monthly or yearly in the metropolis?

....

....

18. What is the average waste per capital per day in the metropolis as at 2016?

....

....

19. What percentage of the populace enjoy the services of waste collection in the metropolis?

....

....

20. Which companies are involved in house to house collection?

....

....

21. Which companies are involved in communal collection?

....

....

22. What is the current process for waste management?

....

....

23. What is the percentage of waste sent to landfill weekly, monthly or yearly?

....

....

24. What percentage of solid waste is recycled weekly, monthly or yearly?

....

....

25. What is the major classification of waste according to KMA?

....

....

26. What are the sources of solid waste I the metropolis?

....

....

27. What is the composition and percentage of solid waste in the metropolis?

....

....

28. What is the rate of waste generation in the metropolis from?

....

....

29. How can waste generation be reduced in the metropolis?

....

....

30. How is waste transferred to dumpsites?

....

....

31. What are some of the recovery and processing strategies in waste management used by the waste department?

....

....

32. Which people are engaged in sorting of solid waste in the metropolis?

....

....

33. How effective is sorting of solid waste in the metropolis and what are the processes involved?

....

....

34. What are the current pertaining challenges and their efforts on waste management curbed?

....

....